Creative Classroom Communications

Creative Classroom Communications

Winifred Currie

GOSPEL PUBLISHING HOUSE
Springfield, Missouri
02-0507

CREATIVE CLASSROOM COMMUNICATIONS

Gospel Publishing House
Springfield, Missouri 65802

This is a Workers Training Division
textbook. Credit for its
study will be issued under Classification 4,
National Sunday School Department,
Assemblies of God.

Printed in the United States of America

Preface

Critics of education declare that there is a crisis in our classrooms today. "Mindlessness" is the word used by one critic to describe the inability of educators to take time to ask *why* they are doing what they are doing; *why* the breakdown of communications between teacher and pupil exists.

The purpose of these pages is to help us as Christian educators to learn God's prescription for improving teaching and learning divine truth by focusing our attention on the meaning and implications of personalized, Christ-centered communications between teachers and pupils.

Some ideas presented may seem strange to you. Yet I hope you will think about them and relate them to your own personal teaching situation whether at home, school, or church. Let us accept Christ's challenge to educate the "now" generation in this difficult age. Part of this acceptance should mean learning from His example what effective, personalized, creative communication really is.

I am indebted to numerous people for the ideas contained in this book. Authors have stimulated my thinking. Students, both in Congo and the United States, have taught me that communicating effectively is not an easy task. Teachers have been sounding boards to my ideas. Some of them have added ideas of their own. The result, I trust, will be of benefit to you, Christian teacher, as your ministry is so important in this crucial decade.

Special acknowledgement is due Joan Goodwin who read the manuscript and offered helpful suggestions. Also I appreciate the typing services of Melodie Smith and Jan Penney.

WINIFRED CURRIE

Contents

1 : Contemporary Christian Communications 7

2 : Communications in Learning 19

3 : Listening to God 31

4 : Listening to People 43

5 : The Credibility of the Communicator 55

6 : Improving Listening Skills 67

7 : Improving Students' Reading Skills 79

8 : How to Speak So Others Listen 92

9 : Aids to Communication 103

10 : Teacher-Pupil Communications 113

Bibliography 123

1 : Contemporary Christian Communications

Modern man seems to be plunging wildly toward a worldwide catastrophe. Many serious thinkers see the danger of society's disentegrating, perhaps in this generation. Population explodes, cities decay, violence increases, pollution spreads. These global problems threaten to destroy mankind, even as man reaches into space, walks on the moon, and speaks to his fellow earthlings from outer space!

What is the prescription for society's ills? One communications expert, Isaac Asimor, prescribes *personalized communications* through television. He envisions that by this means the planet earth will become a cultural unit. Asimor believes that man will be able to take action against the global problems that threaten him. The idea of oneness, fostered by global television's dissemination of information and knowledge, will eliminate fear and hostility among men and direct men's energies toward solutions of common problems.

Although Asimor's remedy for society's ills will be rejected by enlightened Christians because it is based on the philosophy "man can save himself," the prospect of worldwide personalized communications in this decade should not be ignored by Christ's followers. Experts predict that the expansion of communication satellites will make it possible for every person on the earth to press a button on his TV and select the information he wants to have.

Will this advancement mean the demise of mass communication as we now know it, where a few powerful people can control the ideas and information that are communicated to the public? Communications experts like Asimor would say yes. They see the possibility of vast computer centers where tapes and microfiches will make both the spoken word and the printed word accessible to the common man through the medium of his television set. Asimor predicts that people on the banks of the Zambezi as well as on the banks of the Thames or Mississippi rivers will be able to select what they want to see and hear on television. Think of the significance of this development in terms of Christian communications!

Asimor's prediction of the future of personalized, as opposed to mass, communication may be realized in this decade. The use of it as a means for solving society's ills seems unrealistic to Christians. However, Jesus did practice the idea of personalized communication, not in an electronic "press-the-button" sense, but in a spiritual, dynamic sense. The early Christians, obeying His orders, communicated God's message in a highly personalized way to the world of their day. They declared that God's prescription for society's problems was to be found in accepting by faith the "good news" that Jesus Christ is the Messiah, the divinely appointed Saviour, man's Redeemer.

Can Christians today know how to communicate even more effectively in this electronic age? "Greater things than these shall you do," Jesus said to His followers as they marveled at the miracles He performed. Dare we believe that God will do greater things through Christians everywhere in this modern world than He accomplished through the nucleus of dedicated Christians of the first century? God has not changed His message since their day of personalized communications in the ancient world. The Holy Spirit who gave them power to express the gospel without fear is still willing to do the same for Christian believers today. The tools available to us are much more advanced in this technological age. What, then, would hinder us from doing a better job in reaching the billions in the world today?

What must today's Christian know about communicating the Christian message to this rapidly changing world? How can he transmit these ideas, whose truth he knows by experience to be valid, in relevant and effective ways? How can he utilize in the best manner the tools of communication God has made available to him? The message must be personalized as well as adapted to the culture in which he lives. Relevancy and personalization of the gospel to individual needs were Christ's specialities. A study of the field of communications as it exists today, coupled with an understanding of how Christ would personalize and relate the Christian message if He were on earth, should help us to answer these questions.

What Is Communication?

Communication has been defined as the process of transmitting ideas and thoughts from one person to another person or persons. It not only involves discourse, a one-way communication, but dialogue or discussion, a two-way or multichanneled type of communication. In spite of the fact that we use communication so much as normal human beings, we seldom give thought to what the process of communication really is. Sometimes we may be honest enough to admit that we encounter difficulties in expressing our ideas to other persons or in understanding what someone is saying to us. Teachers especially, who are so intensely involved in communication, are apt to assume that the difficulty lies with the receivers of the message. Too frequently they diagnose the student for possible problems in learning and listening rather than taking a closer look also at the medium of communication. A study of the process of communication reveals how complicated the whole area of transmission-reception of ideas is, especially as it involves human beings. As one studies the process, he becomes aware of the many different reasons why a communication may fail.

Characteristics of Communications

First, *communication is uniquely an activity of persons.* Communication of ideas and thoughts from one person to another is one of the distinctive characteristics of people. Animals express their feelings and wants by sounds or actions, but the form of communication involving the mind in the association of ideas into meaningful categories and the expression of these ideas in comprehensible language is a human activity.

George A. Miller of Harvard states in his preface to a collection of essays on communication, of which he is editor, that "no other aspect so clearly separates man from other species of animal, or is the source of so many peculiarly human strengths and weaknesses."

The ability to communicate in language differentiates man from the animal kingdom and develops him as a person. Furthermore, when man learns also how to communicate with God as person to Person, he begins to understand both the horizontal and vertical dimensions of communication. Communion and fellowship on a spiritual plane are then possible and contribute to making that man a *whole* person.

Being a whole person involves more than rising above the animal kingdom in our interchange of ideas with other human beings. It also involves the higher plane of communication intimately with our Creator in the realm of the spirit as person to Person. To be inhibited in this plane brings frustration even more deeply affecting us than the frustration experienced by a deaf-mute child. Being in a world of silence frightens him. When someone in that outside world manages to find a way to break through the wall of silence and involve the child in a meaningful form of communication such as sign language the fear subsides, the frustration dissipates. He knows then that he is a *person,* capable of communicating even though he is handicapped and the channels of communication open to him are limited because of his sensory deficiency. The act of communication, limited as it is, has proved to him that he is someone. He can communicate because he is a *person.*

Second, *communication is a science.* The term science implies that emphasis is placed on the principles governing the phenomenon of persons communicating with one another. The intricate skill involved in transmitting and receiving a message certainly deserves to be classified as a science. Persons who study communications as a science admit that one of the major problems is what they call "noise." This results in a distortion of the message, rendering it unintelligible to the receiver. "Noise" or interference is often physical in origin as, for example, is a "poor connection" on the telephone, or when a student constantly interrupts a teacher or distracts his classmates by disruptive behavior, involving what we now call a form of "noise pollution." Noise may also be linguistic in origin, as when a person transmits a message either vocally or in writing, in a code or language unknown to the receiver.

Jesus, although He did not live on this earth in the electronic age of communications, did demonstrate in His teaching His understanding of the science of communications. He practiced the basic principles of communication between people by choosing quiet countryside or lakeside locations for His most important discourses or dialogues. He was aware that He must speak in the language of the people, using a code familiar to them. He knew that communication to be effective must involve the use of words or a *code* which stood as symbols of important ideas inherent in God's message. In many ways He succeeded in overcoming distracting "noise" by choosing quiet open classrooms whenever possible, by speaking in the code—words familiar to the people—by drawing His illustrations from the everyday life of His listeners, by starting from their point of interest. He talked about the water of life to the thirsty Samaritan woman at the well (John 4), the bread of life to the multitudes whose physical hunger had been satisfied by a boy's lunch of bread and fish (John 6), and the correct priorities of life to the greedy aristocrats of the Jewish church, using a Roman coin (Luke 20:25). Jesus certainly understood the *science of communication*.

Third, *communication is an art*. It involves a perception of the end to be achieved and the means by which this can be attained in a practical manner. It is a skill involving the expression of man's feelings, attitudes, and values as well as his ideas.

Jesus used word pictures to express His ideas. Common everyday life objects were also used to illustrate truth as well as the figurative language of the parable. By these means Jesus helped people to *remember* and *to think about* His teaching. He knew that basic concepts of God's message often were not initially grasped by the hearers, including His disciples, but that the word pictures or context in which He presented the concepts would be remembered by a mental image in the receivers' minds. An example of this would be Jesus' teaching to His disciples about His imminent death and resurrection which they had found impossible to understand or believe. Through the use of the illustration of the seed falling into the ground and dying and then bringing forth much fruit, they later understood why He had to die. They retained the concept of death preceding life through the mental image of the planted seed. After His death and resurrection, additional experience coupled with the strength of this word picture resulted in an understanding of Jesus' initial communication to them.

Communication is also an art because its success or failure depends on the attitudes or mind-set of both transmitters and receivers. If a person wants to communicate effectively, he must be aware of the attitudes and emotional state of his hearers.

The apostle Paul was not only aware of the difficulties which a prejudiced Jerusalem church posed to the reception of his reasons for ministering to the Gentiles; he also knew the *means* which he must employ to assure the attainment of his *goal*. He knew that it was important to the future of the spreading of the gospel among the Gentiles that the mother Christian church at Jerusalem, which was largely Jewish in membership, receive favorably his recommendations. He had to communicate successfully to this key church the burden of his call to minister to the Gentiles.

In Galatians 2:2 Paul tells us how he overcame the psychological "noise" of racial prejudice so that his message came through clearly. He minimized the danger of interference by first of all communicating with the church leaders privately. He presented simply how God had made real to his disciplined Jewish mind (previous to his conversion one of the most prejudiced ones) the truth that the gospel of Jesus Christ was to be declared to the Gentiles in all lands under his apostolic leadership.

Paul was humble enough at that point to recognize his low credibility with the rank and file of the Jerusalem church who still remembered his persecution of Christians before his conversion. By going to the key men of the church and getting them to listen to him, Paul succeeded in neutralizing the effect of racial bias and un-Christlike attitudes on the important decision.

Fourth, communication must be regarded as not only a form of expression (output of ideas) but also as *an act of reception* (input of ideas). Greater emphasis needs to be placed today on the interchange of ideas and opinions through conversation and mutual sharing. People are increasingly more reluctant to receive passively data without questioning the validity of the message. Teachers, preachers, missionaries, writers are apt to be challenged today, especially by skeptical young people. This can be beneficial if open-mindedness and sincerity are maintained by all persons involved in the communication.

Jesus never encouraged gullibility on the part of His audience, involving himself as much as possible in meaningful dialogue or discussion. Feedback, a response to His message, was always important to Him. He not only answered their questions but "read their thoughts," even though these thoughts were expressed in nonverbal ways such as gestures, actions, or facial expressions. An example of this perceptive evaluation of Jesus to His audience's reaction to His teaching is found in the account of the religious leaders' unvocalized response to His startling statement to the paralytic, "Son, your sins are forgiven!" The unspoken criticism of blasphemy was immediately recognized by Jesus and dealt with by healing the afflicted man (Mark 2:5-8). Thus He showed the error of their thinking.

Jesus' conversation with an intellectual, Nicodemus, is recorded in John 3. It is an outstanding example of communication involving both expression and reception. It is also a dynamic example of a personalized, two-way communication concerning the necessity of the "new birth," a truth basic to Christian faith and experience. Think of how many people have read this account of Jesus' and Nicodemus' dialogue and have believed in Christ as the giver of divine life!

Christian Communications

To communicate the Christian message effectively one must understand the basic processes of communication in general. He must also understand that Christian communications are similar to secular communications in process, but they are always distinctive from worldly communication especially in message and purpose.

The *message* of Christian communications is distinctive because its focal point is Jesus Christ. The message states that there is no other name under heaven by which we may be saved (Acts 4:12). It claims that only Jesus can save us from our sinful state and assure us as human beings forgiveness and deliverance from sin and guilt.

The goals of Christian communications are always directed toward persuading men that the message is viable and true. If man believes the message of salvation through Jesus Christ, he receives eternal life as God has promised.

The *model* of Christian communications is Jesus Christ, the great Teacher, the perfect Communicator. Not only did He "tell it as it is," but He showed us how to live this distinctive gospel in this world. He is our model of how to communicate this gospel to others. He spoke without fear or favor, with love and compassion, and people listened to Him because they sensed that He spoke God's message personally to them.

The common people who had lost faith in the established church of their day heard Him gladly. He spoke fearlessly but tenderly and with authority. He had credibility, because He lived what He taught. "Come to Me," He said, "and I will give you rest—all of you work so hard beneath a heavy yoke. Wear My yoke, for it fits perfectly and let Me teach you; for I am gentle and humble, and you shall find rest for your souls; for I give you only light burdens." What a message! What a model!

The message and the model of Christian communications are unchanging and unchangeable. However, the human instruments communicating the message and following the model change because they are human. But God chose this method of communicating to the world. The physical *methods* should change according to the pattern of the changing world in which we live. As Dennett has stated in his interesting book on Christian Communications, human instruments may hinder the ministry of the Holy Spirit in convicting man of sin as the result of hearing God's message. He suggests that failure to reassess every facet of the practical and physical side of communicating the Christian message in this changing world accounts for much of the weakness in Christian communications today. Do we love "the way that we have always done it" so well that we actually hinder rather than help people to find Christ by listening to His message?

This does not mean that Dennett is advocating a blind adoption of so-called "new methods" of communications. A careful *assessment* of these methods in the light of the Christian perspective and the *adaptation* of methods which work in this changing world would certainly seem in order.

It is in this area of flexibility in the context of consistency that the Christian communicator should excel. He has access not only to the latest methods of effective communication but the wisdom of God, who knows the heart of man. Should he not expect that greater things, more lasting behavioral changes should take place in the lives of persons as he communicates God's message than secular communicators could ever realize?

The "Now" Generation

Although the Christian in today's world is called to communicate Christ's gospel to all generations in his contemporary world, the generation that seems to pose the greatest difficulty is the so-called "now" generation. The young people of this generation present a challenge in the entire world today. They are numerous, often rebellious against authority, articulate, and wanting to be listened to by adults. They are searching for identity and reality, disrespectful of the "establishment," including the established church.

This generation wants to know by experience whether or not the message of Jesus Christ is true. Talk to this generation must be honest. Worn-out clichés are rejected. The danger of the Christian communicator is to be distracted by the evidences of the post-Christian culture which this generation represents—the long hair, dirty clothes, obscene language, apparent laziness, and chronic restlessness. Intervention must be *immediate*, *effective*, and *Christ-centered* in order to touch them with the gospel in a language they can understand—the language of God's love for sinful man no matter who he is or how he looks on the outside. The Christian has the only message that can save this "now" generation from destroying itself and "turn them on" for Christ.

Summary

Unprecedented opportunities to communicate Christ's message effectively are available to every Christian who knows by experience as well as by rational faith that the truth of the gospel becomes real to those who listen and accept it by faith. The challenge of our day demands immediate attention to the needs of the troubled world, including the "now" generation. To accomplish this formidable task, God needs communicators who not only understand the process and characteristics of personalized communication, but who know the distinctiveness of Christian communications in message, model, and methods; who can adapt to the troubled, changing world in which they live as Christians. God has indeed the prescription for our society's ills at this crucial time in world history.

2 : Communications in Learning

The first century Christians certainly communicated the gospel of Jesus Christ effectively. Some of them had been taught by Jesus personally. They learned from Him not only the basic concepts of Christian truth, but also how to communicate these concepts to others. These disciples in turn taught other followers of Christ.

On the Day of Pentecost the truths they had learned from Jesus suddenly became startlingly lucid and meaningful to them. The tremendous urge to share this good news with their own generation produced a growing and dynamic community of Christ-followers, who believed that Jesus was the Messiah, Son of God, Saviour of mankind. The Christian Church was born!

For many Christians today communicating God's message as effectively as the early Christians seems to be difficult. Why should this be so? Perhaps an intuitive approach to this question might be more helpful than the logical, problem-solving techniques that modern man is inclined to follow. Instead of analyzing the problem and then prescribing a remedy, let us look at the difficulties of Christian communications from the viewpoint of the learner whom we wish to teach; or the person with whom we desire to converse concerning his spiritual needs.

If we consider how people learn, perhaps we shall then understand more clearly why some persons do not understand the truth of God's message which we are trying to communicate to them. The process of learning is indeed an interesting and helpful study, especially to teachers.

In the past little attention was given to the "receivers," the listeners and readers, who may or may not have understood what a communication was all about. It was much more important to train the "transmitters" (the speakers and writers) in the forms of proper expression, than it was to train the "receivers" to listen and to read properly. It was the breakdown in industrial communications some 30 or 40 years ago that made educators stop and realize that much of what was being communicated in well-polished phrases was not being correctly understood by the "receivers." How many of us, for example, have tried to understand the directions for using some new purchase or to comprehend the directions given orally by a teacher on the steps toward solving some complicated mathematical problem?

The psychologists and linguists have focused their research on the difficulties of reception and have brought into being this new science of communications, with its emphasis on the audience and the readers. According to Dennett, the business world was quick to learn the lesson from this new approach to communication and to profit by it. Have we as educators, Christian workers, missionaries stopped to investigate the extent to which our words have been misunderstood by the "receivers"?

To the Christian educator, the importance of the "receiver" (learner) cannot be overlooked. Can the psychologists, the linguists, and the successful teachers explain to us how the learner really learns? Actually, this is not new, for we find many instances in the Bible of this concern on the part of alert teachers for an understanding reception of God's Word. Philip interrupted the Ethiopian officer as he was reading the 53rd chapter of Isaiah with the question, "Do you *understand* what you are reading?"

However, how many sermons are preached, Bible lessons taught, expositions written, radio broadcasts transmitted, lectures presented without a valid form of feedback to aid in knowing whether or not the hearers or readers learned anything worthwhile!

Today there are many more detractors, more noise pollutants, and greater interference to the transmission of the Christian message than man has ever known. In spite of our advanced technology in communications, the Christian message has to be transmitted in a climate which is hostile to Christian thinking. In fact, many Christian leaders would agree with Schaeffer when, in his book *Death in the City*, he describes the world of today as post-Christian because the Western World culture was built on a Christian consensus, but now we must face the fact that our children are growing up in a society in which the Christian viewpoint is in the minority. Modern man thinks that *nobody* is home in the universe, according to Schaeffer. If we face the significance of this statement realistically we shall at least be more aware of the *great* difficulties involved in communicating God's message in today's world.

Let us then in the context of this observation study one of the most difficult problems encountered by the Christian communicators—the problem of learning.

How We Learn (Reception)

The process of language experience involves the reception of outside stimuli such as words into the brain. The input of data transmitted in the medium of spoken or written expression, as far as concept-building inside the brain is concerned, involves essentially three senses. The message may also be transmitted by movement or by a graphic representation of an actual object. In any event, the reception of the message involves the auditory or hearing, the visual or seeing, and the tactile or touching senses. Data may also be processed to the human brain by a combination of any two or all three of these senses simultaneously.

Modern educational psychology emphasizes that people process information differently. The opinion is quite widely accepted today that each would-be receiver of stimuli has one mode of learning which is the easiest channel for him in processing the ideas, information, and other data from the outside environment. This point will be elaborated further on and the implications evaluated for the teacher who wants to teach so that all of his pupils will learn as much as possible in the assigned time.

Biblical examples of using the auditory sense for learning would be the mighty rushing wind on the Day of Pentecost, the sound of which was heard not only by the 120 in the Upper Room, but by many people in the city. This phenomenon so startled the crowds in Jerusalem that they came running to see what it was all about. When they arrived at the house where Jesus' followers were meeting, they were stunned to hear their own languages being spoken by these disciples from Galilee. Many languages were represented in that diverse crowd gathered there that memorable day for the Feast of Pentecost. These two phenomena were God's means of conveying to them through their auditory senses that a great event was taking place. The spiritual significance of this event was then explained by Peter as he spoke to the amazed crowd and preached to them that Jesus Christ was the Messiah and had sent the Holy Spirit to His servants, men and women alike, so that they might prophesy in His name.

These people learned by hearing just as many persons have done during the history of the human race. However, some people have considerable difficulty learning by *listening* for various reasons. This is clearly understood when a person is handicapped by deafness. It is more difficult to understand when a learner has a perceptual auditory loss so that he does not process language well through listening. This handicap is sometimes called word deafness or other technical names, including a form of aphasia.

God through His prophets often accused the Israelites of being dull of hearing. Isaiah quotes God as saying that they had ears but did not hear because of their unwillingness to listen to God. Jesus described the Jews of His time on earth as having the same spiritual disease—being unwilling or unable to listen and to understand what He was saying to them.

How often have teachers or other speakers been aware of students or members of an audience who are not processing well what is being said to them? We speak of inattentiveness, but do we always realize why some people don't learn much through listening?

The fact, however, is that the great majority of people in the world today acquire a considerable percentage of their new knowledge through the auditory input channel. Children and poor readers especially depend on it for their input of information in school. Most research in this area indicates that the average person remembers only 25 to 50 percent of what he hears.

The second sensory reception area is that of the *visual*. Much learning is acquired through this channel, not only through the medium of the printed page but also through the visual observation of the world around us. The miracles of Jesus were in most cases observable and demonstrated as a sort of object lesson of the reality of His message. John's Gospel contains a striking example of this truth. John recorded how Jesus performed the miracle of healing the blind man and then used this visual demonstration of divine power as the context for communicating the concept that He is the Light of the World, bringing spiritual illumination to those who believe on Him.

Jesus frequently used objects, such as a mustard seed, a fish, a coin, a fig tree, a loaf of bread, a well of water, and a worn wineskin, to teach important truths and to aid learning. God's Word, the Bible, has had a significant influence in spreading God's message since it was first printed by Gutenberg on his printing press in 1458. Today as more and more translations in different languages become available and literacy increases, millions of people have access to this visual input of God's data of divine truth.

Art, photography, and the wonder of the electronic age, television, have resulted in the literal bombardment of modern man's visual sense with data. One must more than ever train himself to be selective in what types of visual data he is willing to expose himself to. For parents, the present problem of monitoring what their children see has become a monumental task. This is particularly important when one realizes that vision is the sense through which the most lasting impressions are made on the mind.

In a later chapter we shall discuss some of the reasons why some children find learning to read very difficult. Because reading is for normal people (excluding the visually handicapped, the blind) a visual act dependent on visual perception, a deficiency in the brain's ability to perceive accurately symbols presented to it through the visual sensory channel is believed to be one of the principal causes of reading disability.

The third sensory reception area is that of the tactile (sense of touch). This sense is especially important to the blind who use it to compensate for their visual handicap in learning to read. However, the sense of touch is also beneficial in learning for almost all "receivers." Children use it considerably during early childhood, especially to develop concepts of space. A very sick woman used it to find healing by touching the hem of Jesus' garment—her faith in Christ's healing power made her well as she touched His clothes. Jesus often touched people to show His love and compassion for them, bringing healing to the so-called untouchables, the lepers of His land, as well as to many other sick people.

Children who are seriously restricted in one sensory area often learn easily through another sense. However, frequently teachers and other communicators forget this fact and assume that all "receivers" learn in the same way as they do. Consequently they are apt to overwork one channel of input to the neglect of the other sensory channels. For example, the communicator who has learned well all his life through the auditory channel (listening) may be inclined to talk too much, assuming erroneously that everyone learns as well as he does through the auditory sense. Learning for some people will be minimal as a result.

Actually electronics as a science has greatly improved the efficiency of communication by using sound-sight (audiovisual) presentations simultaneously to convey knowledge to learners. The multisensory approach to the teaching of reading, involving the visual-auditory-tactile senses, has proved very helpful to children having severe learning disability in reading.

How We Learn (Conceptualizing)

Man has the capacity to transform images received through his senses into meaning, thus adding to his experiences. He is able to develop concepts, to think, to conceptualize. This ability enables one to make sense out of the "messages" coming to his brain from the outside world. The speed and efficiency by which he can do this is often called intelligence, a term frequently misused or abused by educators and parents. Probably it is one of the most misunderstood words in any language.

The conceptualizing capacity of man enables him to select and to respond to key stimuli of the external world. There are thought to be three levels of conceptualizing or generalizing. The first level is the *association* or integration level; the second is called the *convergent* level of conceptualizing; the third, the *divergent* or creative level of thinking.

Associative level. Data coming to the brain through the senses or receptors are identified as meaningful only when the person's mind perceives the relationship of the "new" idea or bit of information to past memories. When a relationship to a past experience can be made, the mind is engaged in categorizing the associated concept in an orderly manner. This is the first level of understanding and is basic to more complex thinking-models. Basic to this generalizing is the ability to perceive correctly the stimuli that have been flashed to the brain through the receptors. As we have already stated in chapter 1, when distortion of the message occurs as a result of outer or inner "noise," the communication to the receiving person is incorrectly perceived and consequently misunderstood. Association or integration of the message into the past experiences or knowledge of the receiver or learner either becomes impossible or inaccurate. The communicator, if he detects the misunderstanding, is liable to complain that his message has been distorted and is inclined to blame the learner. No learning results, of course, because the teacher is unwilling to transmit the message in a different medium that would be intelligible to the receiver.

Patient communicators are always willing to try again. This does not mean repetition of the message in the same way in which it was originally presented, but finding the best way to aid the receiver in correctly perceiving the idea; helping him to make the relationship with past experiences so that a meaningful association is realized. It is this latter step that is often overlooked in communication, especially teaching. We too often assume that all persons have the ability to make associations of the new to the old *without* assistance. This is simply not true.

Jesus certainly helped persons to function well at this first level of conceptualizing. In his dialogue with the Samaritan woman, He started transmitting His message with a familiar experience—drawing water from the village well. He skillfully compared the new idea of the *living* water with the natural water in the well. The living water was a gift of God, quenching the spiritual thirst of any recipient of it perpetually, and so producing eternal life. This tremendous message of freedom and blessing, forgiveness and peace, was joyously accepted by this sinful woman because she understood the new concept of how to receive eternal life through association with a familiar symbolism.

Convergent level. This level of conceptualizing is built upon the associative level and involves the concept of the whole. The emphasis now is on building key concepts from what we know as reality on the basic level. It involves ability to draw conclusions from the data that have been organized into meaningful categories.

The Samaritan woman, using this level of conceptualizing in her dialogue with Jesus, grasped the key concept presented by Jesus, drew her own conclusions from the evidence He gave ("He told me everything which I ever did," she said to the villagers) and believed that He was indeed the Messiah, the source of eternal life.

Divergent level. This is the creative level of thinking which results in applying learned concepts to life involving the flash of illumination, the exciting imagery which every human being was intended by God, the Creator, to experience. The intervention of the Holy Spirit truly illuminates the truth of the new experience in knowing, making the message real and personal. Like the Samaritan woman, we find application of this truth, of who Jesus really is, tremendously satisfying to our personal lives. The Samaritan woman, in thinking beyond the truth that Jesus had presented to her, invited the villagers to come and see for themselves. Intuitively she believed that what Christ had taught her about eternal life He could teach them; what He had done for her, He could do for them. Surely she had learned well what living water really was!

Divergent thinking involves the flight of the imagination beyond the limits of the communicated message. New ideas are born in the mind of the receiver! This is the most personalized level of conceptualizing.

How We Learn (Expression-output)

Just as a body of water in order to remain fresh has to give out as well as take in, so the human being must not just take in ideas, assimilate them, classify them, and reflect on their significance to his personal life; he must share these ideas with others. Such expression reinforces learning and increases the capacity to receive new concepts. It is important to emotional as well as spiritual health.

There are two basic forms of expression or output, verbal or nonverbal. Each is a form of communication by which the receiver or learner expresses to the teacher or to another person what he believes the transmitted message means to him. He thereby becomes involved as a transmitter of ideas, a communicator.

The most commonly used form of verbal expression is speech. This motor activity involves the speech or vocal organs, revealing levels of conceptualizing in terms of knowledge, attitudes, opinions, and values. Jesus said that "out of the abundance of the heart the mouth speaketh." Speech indicates what we are thinking, how we feel about something or someone, whether or not we have really understood what we have heard or read.

New experience becomes more meaningful as one articulates what he has learned. People with speech defects or who are inhibited in speaking by shyness often suffer emotionally. The ability to express oneself orally in an intelligible language is a very important human activity. Opportunities for expression through speech need to be provided as much as possible in every learning situation. We have already discussed the importance given to it in the Scriptures as an integral part of the communication cycle.

The second form of verbal expression is writing. This involves visuomotor coordination, which is difficult for some people. Because it is often used in large classes for a feedback activity in a learning situation, students who write poorly often react negatively to teacher pressure put upon them to express their ideas in writing. Based upon my observations of children with learning disabilities, I believe that a lack of understanding on the part of adults of this difficulty (which is usually a neurological one) causes much disruptive behavior on the part of children or adolescents. By observing the writing rate of children, a teacher can determine how much written work each child can produce in a given segment of time.

For some persons writing is a form of expression which they prefer to speaking. Others find any form of verbal expression difficult and prefer to express themselves in nonverbal ways such as art, handicraft, or gestures.

Emotionally disturbed children frequently cannot communicate in any other form. They find nonverbal expression very therapeutic. Others, not gifted verbally, appreciate opportunities given to them by wise teachers to express their ideas, feelings, and knowledge in other ways more adapted to their nonverbal skills.

Christian teachers should be indeed more sensitive than other teachers to the importance of expressive output in the learning process and to the fact that students differ in the forms of expression they find easiest to use. This simply means that some people learn by doing, others by talking or writing. In any event, we need to remember the words of Jesus when He spoke to the "either-or mentality" of the Jewish religious leaders: "These things ought you to do and not leave the others undone!"

Just as our receptive abilities vary, so do our expressive abilities. However, both input and output are important parts of the process of learning and activities of persons. To the extent that they are developed, life becomes more meaningful especially for the mind open to spiritual truth and disciplined by divine grace and love.

Summary

There are different modes of learning. A perceptive teacher will focus his attention on the learner, capitalize on his receptive strength, or input, using the best approach to communicate God's message to him. Following Jesus' example, he will help his students to develop the highest possible level of conceptualizing Christian truths. He will provide opportunities for feedback (output), adapted to the expressive strengths of his students. Finally, he will encourage persons with whom he is communicating God's Word to receive eternal life by faith, experientially knowing that what they have learned is true.

3 : Listening to God

Schaeffer has said in *Death in the City* that modern man does not believe that God is in His universe. He thinks that there is nobody there. "Nobody to love man, nobody to comfort him, even while he seeks desperately to find comfort in the limited, finite, horizontal relationships of life."

There is no comfort, although man seeks it sincerely. Modern man's urge to know God, to reach upward for Him in a vertical relationship, has been denied. The instinct to know God has been suppressed. Men who deny the existence of God turn to demons while their spiritual hungers remain unsatisfied.

In the midst of it all, God is still speaking in His universe and some men are listening. The solemn warning of the writer of the book to the Hebrew Christians reaches us: "So see to it that you obey Him who is speaking to you. For if the people of Israel did not escape when they refused to listen to Moses, the earthly messenger, how terrible our danger if we refuse to listen to God who speaks to us from heaven!" (Hebrews 12:25, *The Living Bible*).

It is time to listen attentively to God even though we are surrounded by men who deny that He is. He does want to communicate with us. As Christians we must listen to Him, not only to satisfy our instinctive hunger to know Him better everyday, but also that we may understand through the Scriptures what is His message for this troubled world. God must indeed communicate with us, before we, His messengers, can communicate effectively. As we listen to Him, the Holy Spirit will comfort us, illuminate our hearts and minds with love and truth, and give us power to express God's message to our generation.

Why Listen to God?

The history of man shows how easily man loses his way when he turns from God. The barren desert in which man finds himself today is a dramatic witness to this fact. Science was supposed to solve all of his problems, and so materialistic man worshiped at the shrine of secularistic scientism. The result has been futile and disappointing. Man has indeed acquired great knowledge of the universe but his faith in scientism has not saved him. Society has not been transformed, as the crime statistics show. As Carl Henry has stated, man needs God in spite of the fact that the science laboratory can produce a mechanical brain. Only the divine Spirit can shape a regenerate heart. Overdependence on man's wisdom has provided only quantitative answers but has not solved man's sin problem. Only God can do that.

Man must turn from his gods, including his dependence on his own wisdom and knowledge, and turn to God, who is the source of true knowledge and wisdom. In listening to the Creator as He speaks to us through His holy Word, we know that we have discovered the true source of truth. We then understand that salvation no longer has to be purchased by our puny deeds but has to be *communicated* to lost man.

God has commanded us to listen to Him. His prophets warn us to beware of dullness and deafness in responding to God's message (Isaiah 6:10; Matthew 11:15). The last book of the Bible contains frequent admonitions by

Christ to the Christian Church, urging it to listen to the message of the Spirit in these last days. Will we obey?

God touches us through His Word as language reaches out to touch others. Only His Word is used to reveal to us spiritual truths that no one else could ever teach us. His Holy Spirit opens our minds so that we perceive that Christ is the power of God, the wisdom of God, who is indeed the answer to man's problems.

As Christians take time to have communion with their Creator, He reveals His plan for this universe; and man is certainly an important part of that plan. There is Somebody in this universe. He is God—to be loved and enjoyed by repentant, searching man! In fact, as man opens his heart to God, he discovers that God has been searching for him. He never tires in His quest.

Modern man prides himself upon his open-mindedness. Yet he refuses to examine God's data in which God reveals himself. God speaks in these last days through His Son, the Scriptures say, but does modern man accept the challenge to listen to the evidence that Jesus is the Son of God? The Gospel of John was written expressly that man might *know* that Jesus is indeed God's Son. The skeptics are challenged by God to read it. Are they listening?

The Christian, who has listened and knows that Jesus is the Son of God, the only name in the universe which can save from sin and judgment, must communicate this message in love. The mission of the church of Christ is the same as Christ's except that Christ came to seek and to save the lost. The Church is commissioned to seek the lost and announce to them that Christ is Saviour. This is the good news.

Listening to God should always precede attempts to communicate this good news of salvation. Peter and the 120 believers waited on God until they heard from Him. The Holy Spirit spoke *through* them on that Day of

Pentecost after God had spoken *to* them, removing their inhibitions, fears, and doubts. They then freely expressed to unbelievers that day what God had communicated to them by His Spirit. They commenced a pattern of behavior which persisted in the early Christian Church—waiting on God in prayer and worship until their hearts were aglow with His love. Then they went out into their world to communicate God's message to others.

Paul went to Arabia to wait on God after his conversion to Christ's way. During that time of listening and waiting he "tuned in" to God, perceiving and conceptualizing the great doctrines of the Christian faith. Later, by speaking and writing he communicated these doctrines to multitudes of people. Through a long and fruitful ministry, Paul taught God's truth. By his inspired writings, God gave to future generations a great portion of the New Testament. How many people through the centuries since the Christian Church was born have been blessed by this communicator of divine truth who took time to listen to God!

How to Listen to God

When we read God's Word, the Bible, God speaks to us. The more we read and study the Scriptures as born-again children of God, the better we understand what the family of God really is. God speaks to us as a father, sometimes instructs us, telling us what is true and what is wrong in our lives. At other times He speaks to encourage us, teaching us to look at the signs of His work in the world rather than to dwell too frequently on Satan's work. He straightens us out, in other words, disciplining us in love, inspiring us to live balanced, joyful lives for His glory. How does He do this? The experience of Christians, who are very aware of this family of God relationship, indicates that He does it mainly through His Word.

Many devoted Christians through the ages have heard God speak audibly to them in various circumstances and places. Sometimes, like Samuel, they have been awakened from sleep by His voice or, like Israel, they have been startled by His voice thundering from a mountaintop. Sometimes He speaks in quietness as He did to Elijah, or in sternness as He did to Saul on his way to persecute the Christians in Damascus. Many Christians today attest to hearing God speak to them, especially in the midst of persecution and suffering.

Renewed emphasis on the ministry of the Holy Spirit even in the so-called established churches has produced greater freedom among believers in Christ for exercising the gifts of the Spirit, including the gift of prophecy. As God speaks through His messengers, inspired by His Holy Spirit, the messages will always be in harmony with the Word of God, the Holy Scriptures. The Holy Spirit does not contradict himself so that the Christian Church should not fear permitting and even encouraging the ministry of the expressive gifts of the Spirit, as long as those words of prophecy are judged by the criteria clearly stated in the Bible.

For every Christian there is the opportunity to hear God's voice in the hour of personal meditation, as so ably expressed by Antoinette Goetschius in her poem entitled "Meditation":

> When I am sore beset I seek some quiet place,
> Some lonely room or barren, windswept hill,
> And there in silence wait alone until
> I see again the smile upon God's face.
> I feel His presence fill me like the dawn
> And hear once more His whispered, "Peace be still,"
> And know again the strength to do His will,
> I turn to take my load and find it gone.

God has taught us in His Word that we must listen

to Him with an open, unprejudiced mind and yielded will. This is the proper spiritual mind-set which removes the danger that the message might be distorted or disregarded. We cannot really listen to God unless we are willing to do so. The major point that the Christian communicator must always remember here is that if he wants people to listen to God's message as he relays it, he must first learn really to listen to God.

Moses had to learn to listen to God before he could lead his people out of the slavery of Egypt. Before he learned this lesson, he tried impulsively to do God's work his way—the way Moses as a young prince thought that it should be done. He was wrong, of course, and had to escape for his life to the desert. It took him 40 years there before God spoke to him from the burning bush. It was God's time and God's method. Moses listened then with humility to God's call.

Are we so busy doing things—legitimate things—for God, that we do not have time to listen to Him? Elijah was so busy defending his faith in God against the idolaters on Mount Carmel that he forgot to take time to gain perspective, to see events as God saw them in the nation of Israel. Elijah became completely discouraged and so depressed that he wanted to die. In the solitude of the wilderness God spoke to him so that he understood what God's plan was and where he fitted into it. He arose a wiser person that day and returned to Israel without fear of the wicked queen Jezebel. He completed his earthly ministry in a cloud of glory and victory!

God is a Person and because He is, He speaks to man, as the Bible clearly states. Daily He speaks through His written Word, through people who love Him, through the voice of our conscience, through the voice of the prophet inspired by the Holy Spirit, through the stillness of the quiet time of prayer and worship. He has used angels, burning bushes, flaming mountains, and dumb animals as instruments of His communications. Sometimes it takes a shipwreck, an accident, an earthquake, a flood, or other so-called "acts of God" to get our attention. He wants us to know that there is *Someone* at home in the universe and that He has a plan for each person whom He has created.

God wants us to know also that He is working in the hearts of men in spite of the moral and spiritual pollution in which man finds himself. God is busy building His "beautiful society," the Church of Jesus Christ. He wants us to know that what matters today is not the consensus of the society in which we live but His will, His message, His plan. He tells us that we must exalt the Person of Christianity, Jesus Christ, and not our opinions or petty ideas. When we are denouncing others, we are not announcing Christ, as E. Stanley Jones has so aptly said. As we take time to listen to God, all of these truths become real to us. We see things as God sees them, and the world cannot press us into its mold of thinking. We become new and different people, able to communicate God's message without embarrassment or fear.

God has also given to His people the right to listen to Him in order that they might not only communicate the good news of salvation to sinners, but also communicate through teaching and guidance the whole, unadulterated truth of God to believers. For this task He gives gifts such as the gifts of teaching, of preaching, of wisdom, of administration for the purpose of developing the beautiful society of God. These gifts to be effective must be based on a sound and thorough knowledge of the Word of God. We must avoid an overdependence on man's wisdom, man's power, and his techniques. Scientific methodology can accomplish many things, but it cannot provide spiritual judgments of what is right or wrong in God's sight. Only

God can enable redeemed man to *know* what is morally and spiritually right.

Redeemed persons, chosen and gifted by God to lead in the church of Christ, must be taught by God in order to teach others. They must be convinced that in Christ man can find the image of the invisible God. He is the model of "rightness," our behavior pattern, the Word of God made flesh, successfully living and expressing the image of God among men.

At the outset of the "Jesus Movement," leading evangelical journals such as *Christianity Today* and *Eternity* stated that it is one aspect of a worldwide spiritual revolution. In fact the great world revival that many students of the Bible believe is predicted as coming in the last days may be at hand, according to Dr. Robert E. Coleman, Asbury College professor. The spiritual revolution will prepare the way for the return of Christ even at the same time that the forces of evil consolidate their power and prepare for the coming of the Antichrist.

As one considers the tremendous challenge of the present, the role of the Spirit-filled Christian seems to be more important than ever it has been. On the one hand he hears everyday of the increasing crime rate, of the astounding problem of alcoholism in the United States, of the epidemic of drug usage and sex promiscuity among the young. On the other hand he hears of the rapid growth of the Jesus Movement, the revivals in Korea, Indonesia, Africa, and South America. What will his reaction be?

Will he become depressed when he feels the increasing aggressiveness of the evil world in which he lives and say like Elijah, "It is enough; now, O Lord, take away my life; for I am not better than my fathers." Will he lament his inability to cope with the sinful situation of his land? Or on the contrary will he hear the voice of the Lord saying, "Go . . . and make disciples . . . baptizing them . . . and then teach these new disciples to obey all the commands which I have given you"? (Matthew 28:19, 20). This is not the time to be depressed but to go and communicate God's message to sinful, rebellious people. Could it be that the rapid spread of the Jesus Movement indicates that this confused, troubled, and corrupt generation *is* hungry for God?

On the other hand one might misread the signs of the spiritual revolution in the world and become overly optimistic. Overoptimism can be dangerous and lead to hasty, premature actions on the part of naive Christians. Listening to God, waiting His time and knowing His way, moving forward at His command—this is the behavior recommended for God's messenger. God will show us His way as we tarry before Him and sincerely restrain all impulsive desires "to get on with the job," regardless of whether we know the correct way to do it or not. Remember that Peter and some of the others probably were anxious to obey Christ's orders to go into all the world, but He told them that first they must return to Jerusalem (of all places, where they crucified Jesus!) and tarry there until they received the infilling of the Holy Spirit.

It would seem that Spirit-filled Christians should be able to listen to God in these days and know how to help the Jesus people, for example, find love and fellowship in Christ's Church, to avoid fanaticism by searching the Scriptures, watching and praying, and consulting with other members of God's unique family. As Michael Harper has warned in his book on the Pentecostal Movement among the established churches, signs and wonders should not be expected unless strict obedience to the will of God is forthcoming. Guidance in this confused world can be realized only by allowing time to wait upon God.

There are always dangers inherent in learning how

to listen to God. One can become too subjective and fanatical, demanding emotional "highs" without responsibility. The Corinthian Church in Paul's day had to be rebuked for their pride in allowing fanaticism to exist in their church meetings. Another danger is divisiveness by which the revived church can be detracted from its major goal of communicating the gospel. Devisiveness is a danger caused by lack of love, as Paul clearly perceived. To counteract it, he wrote that marvelous chapter on love (1 Corinthians 13). He called it the greatest gift of all. If the gifts of the Spirit are operating within the framework of love, there will be no division in the body of Christ, and God will be able to communicate His will in a climate of acceptance and humility.

When to Listen to God

Revelation 3:20 teaches us that there is an opportune time to listen to God. Jesus takes the initiative by seeking to attract our attention, to speak to us, to have fellowship and communion with us. If we respond at His time and heed His voice, we shall really know Him, not only as our Saviour but as our faithful Friend. God speaks of the opportune time not in respect to age but in terms of *when He* extends His invitation to accept Christ.

Often God speaks to man before a crisis period in order to prepare or to ready him for understanding an important concept as He did to Peter before He asked him to go as His messenger to Cornelius' house. Otherwise Peter would never have accepted Cornelius' invitation (according to Jewish law Jews were forbidden to eat with Gentiles) to come to his house to instruct his household in the Christian faith. Acts 10 explains how God talked to Peter and helped him to overcome his racial prejudice. A tremendous blessing came to Cornelius' house as souls were saved and filled with the Holy Spirit as the result of Peter's ministry.

God speaks often when His people need courage or a new sense of direction. He ministered to the weary prophet Elijah when he desperately needed encouragement to continue the battle against idolatry in Israel.

True friendship with God should be developed daily by regular times of fellowship with Him. A time of devotions, as it is frequently called, seems to many a strange occupation of time in this busy, secular world. It proves especially valuable, however, to the child of God who has cultivated the art of prayer, praise, meditation on God's Word, and listening to God.

The habit of having a quiet time in a sanctuary dedicated to God enhances piety and often brings healing of soul or mind. Hannah tarried in the sanctuary to pray from the anguish of her heart for a son. God heard her prayer, rewarded her faith and made it possible for her to give birth to a son, whom she named Samuel. Happiness for her was being a mother. She shared her happiness with God and loaned Samuel to Him for His work. A genuine example of true motherhood was thus recorded in the Bible to the praise of God. God spoke to her as she prayed in the sanctuary, assuring her that her prayer would be answered. Eli, the backslidden priest, was the instrument God had to use to speak to Hannah. She went away happy because in her heart she knew that God had spoken to her.

Jesus zealously protected the sanctuary when He drove out the money changers and merchants from the temple at Jerusalem. He denounced them in righteous indignation because they had turned the house of prayer into a den of thieves. God's house is to be a place where God meets with His people or where sinners go to call on Him for mercy and forgiveness. When we are in the sanctuary, we will benefit greatly by being quiet before God and listening to Him, shutting out the world and the pressures of daily living, taking time to inhale deeply of the fresh air of His presence as He speaks to us.

A modern-day example of God's servants who have learned to listen to God and to dare to obey Him is Brother Andrew, God's Smuggler. Brother Andrew is known internationally as a fearless, devoted servant of God being used to supply Bibles to Christians behind the Iron and Bamboo Curtains. The book written by the Sherrills telling of Brother Andrew's daring ventures of faith shows how intimately he communicates with God and ascertains His divine will.

Summary

E. Stanley Jones wrote: "Father, I see that my silences count. Help me to know the *art* of listening to Thee. Out of these silences may I come with power and love, *to* love men to Thee. Amen."

The base of effective communication with God is the experience of perceiving and knowing God's truth and will. One can only have this experience by taking time to listen to God, to be receptive to His ideas and His commands.

If we believe that God is at home in His universe we shall not refuse to listen to God who speaks to us from heaven. As we listen to Him, we know that only He can regenerate man, opening his understanding and spiritual ears to listen as God's plan for man is revealed. God speaks through His Word as we wait before Him, showing us His hidden truths which we must understand before we can communicate His message to others. Today as the forces of Satan seek to overwhelm us let us learn the art of listening to God, obediently, humbly, and patiently.

4 : Listening to People

In order to communicate God's message effectively, the transmitter (messenger) must know the Source of the message, God, and develop the habit of listening to Him daily through the study of His Word and prayer. He must also take time to let the Holy Spirit interpret for him the truth of God's message, integrating God's ideas into his experience and philosophy. Adapting the message to the times in which he lives, he is able to conceptualize God's ideas without distortion and see their important relevance to the problems of society. This happens as redeemed man listens to God.

The transmitter must also realize that as his heart and mind are saturated with God's truth, unchanging and yet relevant, he must not then assume that he can communicate effectively with others. There is now the question of the receiver of the message. His spiritual and emotional needs must be recognized. It is not enough to think only of his linguistic and intellectual needs and adjust the communication accordingly. For it is not sufficient to speak in the language understood by the hearer or at the level of understanding at which he functions. This is part of the skill of communicating simply the message which will be discussed in another chapter. His other needs as a person must also be known if the communication is to be received with the desired effect.

These emotional and spiritual needs become apparent

as the communicator listens attentively and lovingly to what the receiver or hearer is trying to express to him. In other words, the would-be communicator, whether teacher, preacher, parent, or friend, must train himself to listen and to observe the responses, verbal or nonverbal, of the one to whom he wishes to transmit the message of God.

Thus the communicator must become a careful and attentive listener, tuning in to what the student, audience, child, or friend is really saying. He is not distracted by the person's speech, dress, hair style, gestures, or mannerisms. He listens selectively and prayerfully, striving to perceive the person as he really is—and as God sees him. As the masks drop off (for the need to defend himself is gone) the real person emerges. At that point the messenger of God can rely on the Holy Spirit to give the right word or Scripture from the storehouse of the communicator's knowledge. The message is appropriate and individualized now, used by God to bring to that person just what is needed to meet his spiritual and emotional needs. This type of communication will be remembered and, if the person wills to believe it, will bring forth fruit in his life.

Why Listen to People?

Everyone, even a small child, has a need to be listened to just as he has a need to express himself. People who live in an industrialized society in which great emphasis is placed on human productivity in work and ideas find it difficult to find time to listen to persons like their children who are not directly involved in their parents' workaday world. Many parents come home at the close of a day's work and find other problems demanding their attention. Sad to say, they have little time to listen to Sally tell of her accident at school or hear of Tom's fight with the boy down the street. However, emergencies of this type have to be dealt with, the spouse says; so the weary father listens carelessly and impatiently to Sally's story, quickly makes a judgment about it, and then turns to Tom. By this time the entire communication system of the family is about to break down, with Sally in tears and Tom going out and slamming the door.

Teachers confront the same problems in finding time to listen attentively to the disruptive child at a private conference time after a tiring school day. Children today in our highly urbanized and mobile society are often victims of broken homes, moving from a familiar, friendly environment to a strange, hostile one. They bring this feeling of lostness and loneliness into our classrooms. What do we do about it? Is there time given for the new child to express how he feels to someone who will listen to him? Perhaps at first he may only feel free to draw a picture of how he feels. For a teen-ager, appointing someone from his own age group to talk with him may be the correct gesture. Adults are often lonely, too, and appreciate being listened to by a friendly teacher.

The family conversation at the table one evening was very rudely interrupted by one of the children saying in a loud voice, "Pass the butter!" There was a shocked silence, followed by a rebuke by the parent, resulting in the boy's having to leave the table. A tape recorder happened to be turned on during the entire meal because it was a special get-together of relatives with the family. Later in talking with the child, the father discovered that the boy insisted that he had asked several times for the butter. So the tape recorder was replayed. In the middle of the adult conversation a childish voice was heard saying, "Please, pass the butter." No one heard him. The conversation continued. A louder, childish voice said, "Would someone pass the butter?" No response was heard. Finally an angry, frustrated child's voice could be heard above the conversation, saying, "*Pass the butter!*" followed by the hushed silence and the rebuke. The tape recorder had vindicated the boy's testimony.

Young people today often complain that no one of the older generation listens to them. Sometimes this complaint is justified when it is evident that conversation of a meaningful nature between parents and their adolescents does not exist in many houses today. It is then that a home becomes a house from which the rebellious youth wants to escape. Christian parents and teachers, who represent the adult world in the teen-ager's eyes, should be expected to show a better example of knowing how to listen to young people than secular adults do. The communications channels must be kept open if at all possible.

Adolescents especially are often very troubled by the many decisions they have to make while trying to emerge from the dependency of childhood to the independence of adulthood. They have many anxieties and fears which are often concealed under rebellious exteriors. It is at this point in their lives that they need the firm understanding and guidance of an adult who cares for them enough to be frank with them and to take time to listen to them seriously. Conferences or just plain quiet times of listening to the troubled adolescent as he tries to develop his own values, make his own decisions, and determine his own destiny can be a great blessing if Christ becomes the controlling influence of the conference.

Listening to anxious, guilty adults can sometimes take a great deal of time. The loneliness, despair, and hopelessness of many adult city dwellers presents a great social problem of our industrialized society. Loneliness and anxiety seem to be characteristics of many societies today, especially where affluence is prevalent and individualism has been overemphasized. Responses to telephone ads and radio talk shows are popular partly because some people just want to hear another human voice. Think of the opportunities for Christians to make themselves available for this type of ministry, not only to the prodigals who are reaching out to God, but to aged and sick Christians as well.

Why do you think so many people write to *Dear Abby?* Don't you think that if more Christian ministers, teachers, laymen and women, as well as parents took more time to listen to people's troubles and burdens, Abby, Ann, and the psychiatrists would be less busy?

Jesus set the example and showed us that listening to people was important. Think of His patience with His disciples when they talked about their ambitious plans for their future, believing that Jesus would make them important people in His earthly kingdom. He saw that the cross, not a crown, loomed in the immediate horizon of His life. The disciples saw the crown, prestige, and glory, *not* the cross. Jesus listened to them and then tenderly rebuked them. Later they understood how foolish they had been, but Jesus had not cut them off, ignored their lack of insight, or refused to listen to their requests, foolish as they were. Jesus' disciples were often slow in learning what Christ was teaching them but He always took time to instruct them, involving them in dialogue, listening as well as speaking to them.

Jesus had time to listen to the children who clamored for His attention; the young man with prestige and money who posed that important question about eternal life; the confused religious leader, Nicodemus, who had no idea what being "born again" meant. Jesus knew that by listening to these persons express their needs, He would be more successful in arousing their attention and interest in the spiritual truths He wanted to teach them. He is indeed our model of the perfect Communicator.

The Art of Listening

The art of listening to God has to be cultivated in order for God's children to grow spiritually. The art of listening to other people, some of whom may be demanding or boring, seems for some of us even more difficult to cultivate. However, we learn the art by practicing it deliberately. The ear has to be trained to listen selectively in today's world and to detect quickly people who should be listened to.

We learn to listen with discernment, knowing what is true and what is false, but accepting the conversationalist as a person. Paul Tournier, the Swiss psychiatrist and author, has helped many Christian people by his wise counseling. He has trained and disciplined himself to listen, as his writings clearly indicate.

Discernment, as the Bible teaches, is a gift of God, especially as it is used in keeping order in the church worship services. Persons like Dr. Tournier, because of their training, experience, humility, and empathy, are able to listen with great insight to what a patient is saying. They are very aware that God has the prescription for healing distressed minds and broken hearts, as Jesus said (Luke 4:18, 19). But they also know that the key to healing is correct diagnosis, of which the compilation of significant data is an important part. Listening is one of the most beneficial ways of securing this information.

Teachers need to listen to their students as much as possible to understand the experiences they have encountered during the week. Because the time spent in Biblical instruction is so limited, a wise Christian educator will realize the importance of knowing each student as well as he can. Communication of spiritual truths will be more purposeful, applicable, and personalized by that teacher who has grasped the significance of the experiences, interests, and needs of his students.

Our listening shows we care for the person who is trying to express how he feels or what he thinks. We need to encourage it not only on a personal plane, but also in providing opportunities for students to react to what we are teaching them. Obscure points are easily detected when time is given to clarify the thinking of the receivers. Often we have failed to communicate God's message adequately to someone simply because we missed the distress cues raised by the other person (like the boy at the dinner table). There was a need which had to be met before attention to our message could be given.

I remember occasions when I was trying to teach Congolese students and nothing seemed to be "getting through" to them that day. One cause of inattentiveness I knew was hunger, easily detected because of the listlessness of the class. A few quick questions and the need was verified; they were hungry because someone who had the kitchen duty had failed to prepare the breakfast on time. In rural Congolese schools, some teachers complained to me that the commuting children often came to school without eating because their parents and other guests had "cleaned the cupboard" the previous night! What would you do with that problem? The only solution was to see that a snack was provided, and then get on with the lesson. Later more definite plans were made in an attempt to avoid a recurrence of the problem. You just can't expect hungry people to learn! Jesus knew that and fed the multitude, using a boy's lunch. If He had sent them away hungry, they would have forgotten everything He had taught them that day. They certainly would never have listened as attentively as they did to His discourse on the Bread of Life. Even though many did not grasp the spiritual truth of what He taught them as it is recorded in John 6, they did not forget what He said.

Because of the pressure of modern living, more and more teachers say that listening is a lost art. Sometimes they themselves are so preoccupied with their own personal needs that they cannot take time to listen to a needy student, neighbor, or friend. Consequently the teacher blames the students and the students blame the teacher for the breakdown in communication.

Everyone of us needs someone to listen to us. Superintendents, principals, pastors, and other administrative personnel need to realize that teachers need to be listened to also. Perhaps the rapidly spreading interest in small Bible study and talk-it-over discussion groups is an indication of how much modern Christians feel the need of sharing informally their ideas, problems, and common interests. They want to have understanding fellow Christians listen to them, and they in turn want to learn to listen prayerfully to others.

The art of listening will help us lead souls to Christ because it will prevent us from overloading listeners with words they cannot understand. It can help us to know how to communicate Christ's caring and acceptance of them as sinners. The language of the caring heart has reached out to touch them as we have become aware of their needs through listening.

Some Suggestions for Listeners

A time and a place for listening to someone privately often has to be provided. Sometimes the teacher has to take the initiative in inviting the student to a conference. The objective of the conference should not be motivated by a desire to snoop into a child or teen-ager's private life. It should be primarily to gain information that will help to solve a need which the person has. Some children mistrust adults because in their past experiences adults have abused or deceived them. Most children trust their teachers when they enter school if their preschool experiences with their parents have been stable and accepting. Of course the distrustful child will be the one who needs most desperately to talk to a patient, loving teacher, but he will find it very difficult to do so. The wise adult in this case will let that child take the initiative in talking, waiting patiently for the troubled child to share his fears, hostilities, and anxieties. Sometimes professional help will be needed for this type of child. But in any event the prayerful teacher must not give up committing the child to God.

Sometimes it is the quiet, withdrawn child who needs the attention of the parent or teacher the most. It is not always the attention-getter child or teen-ager who has the deepest need for someone to listen to him. However, individual conferences for *every* person in your home or class are important. The mother of John and Charles Wesley had a large family, but she always managed to have a private time with each child periodically. This should be a regular practice in every Christian home, especially as the pressures of modern living mount and problems surround our children. It should be a time when the child has the full attention of the adult and interruptions can be avoided as much as possible. Confidences, however small, should be carefully guarded and honored.

I believe that this type of personal conference should be encouraged and fostered in the church also. The depersonalizing characteristic of the world in which our children and teen-agers live needs to be counteracted by the purposeful personalizing of the gospel which Jesus taught and practiced. The most convenient place and method for the contact should be sought. Increasingly the church is being used (rightly so, when one considers the great investment of money put into our modern churches and educational plants) as a sanctuary for people who have a need to be listened to. It is often easy to make the next step, guiding the person into committing his problems to God and listening together for His counsel and guidance.

The art of listening involves follow-up. Sometimes this part of the art leads to the person who has been expressing himself to the teacher or counselor, to reach outside of himself to Christ and find the horizons of his formerly restricted, ego-centered life suddenly expanded. Life then appears as beautiful and worth living. The wise teacher or parent supports this flight of the newborn child in Christ by being accessible when he or she is needed to encourage and to instruct. However, he supports not dominates, never trying to do the student's learning for him.

This skill of being supportive in the follow-up to a beneficial listening session, conference, and commitment to Christ is illustrated by the experience of E. Stanley Jones with a Hindu businessman who had attended an Ashram (deeper-life conference) in India. Mr. Jones and the Hindu had a personal conference of an hour together. Afterward this businessman said, "I went away walking on air, not touching the earth." That hour together cemented the hearts of the teacher and student. The next day, Mr. Jones and he marched in procession together, singing the processional hymn, but the newborn Christian was out of tune. What did Stanley Jones do along with the other experienced Christians around him? They sang louder than his out-of-tuneness, so they marched along without a break. The converted Hindu was expressing his newfound joy badly, but *he was expressing it*. By loving him and accepting his out-of-tune expression, the Christians knew that he would stay around long enough eventually to catch the tune and learn to express himself in Christian music that was acceptable. What a lesson for us to think about in learning to be efficient, loving communicators for Christ, an important part of which is to be supportive in listening follow-up! We must encourage expression from our children and our students, even though it may often be imperfect.

Keeping in touch with those people for whom we have responsibility takes time, planning, tact, and caring. It involves making oneself accessible to people, reaching out to them in caring, encouraging them to express themselves in a class, small group, or individual conferences. Listening, then, becomes an art which we carefully practice, following the example of Christ who taught us how to personalize our listening.

Summary

As teachers, parents, friends, or other communicators, we need to learn the art of listening to others so that communication becomes a two-way channel, meaningful to all parties engaged in the interchange of language. Everyone, even the small child, has a need to be listened to, so that his inner thoughts and feelings may be expressed.

Attentive listening shows that we care for the person who is speaking, recognizing that he is important to us and that he is learning by our careful listening to what his needs are. Listening provides knowledge about persons so that as Christians we can communicate God's message in a more meaningful, relevant manner. Through listening the communicator (teacher, parent, pastor, etc.) becomes aware of the emotional and spiritual needs of the receiver (student, child, parishioner, etc.). Listening helps people to overcome their loneliness and feeling of being unwanted.

It is an art that needs to be developed in the home, church, and school under the personalized instruction of Christ's example as taught in His Word. He knew how to listen to people.

5 : The Credibility of the Communicator

A communicator must be credible; otherwise his efforts to communicate will be useless. In other words, people must have confidence in him as a witness of the truth, as one who knows experientially what he is talking about.

There is a high degree of skepticism in the world today. Young people especially seem more skeptical than in any previous generation. They often do not believe an adult because they have believed the myth of the generation gap. Thus they have lost confidence in authority figures: parents, teachers, ministers, police, and politicians.

The poor distrust the prosperous. The prosperous often doubt that the poor can do anything to help themselves. The poor do not believe the rich because they feel that they will be oppressed or taken advantage of by them. We have the gap between the haves and the have-nots. This is called the poverty gap.

The Vietnam conflict has caused lack of credibility in the military leaders of our country by the peace people or doves. The people who believe in the threat of worldwide Communism to our national security have no confidence in the doves, feeling that they are weakening our country and encouraging the Communists to take over the government. The doves mistrust the hawks, accusing them of supporting military aggression. Meanwhile many people of the "now" generation believe that all of these gaps actually exist and refuse even to listen to people connected with the "establishment," far less believe them. That is one of the reasons why there is such rootlessness among some of the young today. They refuse to accept the guidance of the adults who have been sent to guide them. Others listen but are often very skeptical of what concerned adults are trying to say to them.

The mass media unfortunately have encouraged some of this skeptical attitude on the part of the young, fostering the generation, economic, racial, and other so-called gaps in our society. Society is now fragmented so seriously that many leaders despair of its healing. That is why men talk of world government, world communication, a world leader as the only means of saving society.

As a result, the Christians, who seek sincerely to communicate God's message of salvation to the lost, often face formidable barriers. They find it extremely difficult to minister to the young as well as adults, the blacks as well as the whites, the poor as well as the rich, the doves and the hawks.

This question of credibility is indeed serious, because a message will be accepted by the receiver only if it is believed. Research indicates that the degree of credibility the receiver bestows upon the transmitter of the message determines the proportion of his acceptance of it. A message itself can also lack credibility for certain hearers especially if it is a threat to their security or is *perceived* by the listener as a threat to the status quo.

A teacher to be listened to must then be believed if the message is to be productive and result in changed behavior of the hearers or receivers. A prophet to be heard must be credible, possessing the credentials that convince people God has chosen him to bring His message for this time and people. Also there are some who refuse to believe a prophet's word, even though they are convinced that God has sent him. It is really the message which they reject. This was the situation of Isaiah and Jeremiah. The backslidden nation did not want to believe the message of judgment which they preached—namely, the captivity of the people in Babylon, their subjugation to foreign armies, and the destruction of Jerusalem. How many messages of impending judgment are being preached today? If there are bold prophets who preach a message of repentance and judgment who believes them?

Evidences of Credibility

When a communicator is listened to attentively by an audience and his lecture or address is not punctuated by protestors shouting obscenities at him, one would probably say in this confused world, "He is credible!" However, tyrants have been heard and their messages accepted by people who have been deluded by their oratory or unusual gift of persuasion. Many world leaders who hold dictatorial powers over their people have high credibility in the eyes of the deluded ones. The Bible foretells that this type of delusion will be widespread in the world before the Antichrist appears. In fact, the Antichrist will probably have the highest degree of credibility among the ungodly that anyone has ever had or will ever have because Satan's deception will be behind him.

However, people who really seek to know the truth of God and obey it will know that truth, believe that message is from God, when they hear it. The hungry souls who really want to know God will recognize the Bread of Life as genuine when Christ is presented to them. In order to be credible, the messenger, then, must truly believe God's message and show by his life that he practices its precepts and concepts. The world today will turn off the transmitter who doesn't practice what he speaks, teaches, or preaches of divine truth. The rank and file seem to be much more ready to discover the hypocrisy among so-called Christians than they are among atheistic professors or ranting demagogues.

Be that as it may, the true communicator of Jesus' gospel will always strive to achieve credibility by his love for Christ, by his works, his practical faith, and the evidence of the fruits of the Spirit in his life. The hearers then show respect for this type of communicator even though they may not always agree with everything he says from the Word of God.

The response to the communicated message is respectful, enthusiastic, and positive when the messenger is a credible person in the Christian faith. The receivers are not threatened by the message because it is given in love and they know that it is the truth. Think of the high credibility of John the Baptist among the common people even though he called them to repentance. Their mind-set to God was favorable; they wanted to believe, to become different persons. They knew John the Baptist was a prophet sent by God because their hungry spirit told them that his message was real. He was highly credible with them, but he had low credibility with the religious leaders of the Jews. His message offended them; it was too crude. His way of life was too ascetic, his dress too simple. They did not want to believe him because the message of repentance and the coming of the Messiah were too threatening to their theology and their training. In many cases the message threatened them because of their political misdeeds and their power over the established Jewish church.

Jesus himself had low credibility with the religious leaders of His day because of his lowly social status and inadequate educational credentials. However, it should be noted that honest leaders like Nicodemus were willing to believe Jesus' teachings and eventually to follow Him, having been impressed by His power and love.

It is indeed a shame when a messenger has lost his credibility among persons who really want to know the truth. The truth is rejected simply because the transmitter has shown by repeated inconsistent behavior or other reasons why he cannot be trusted.

Causes of Low Credibility

There are many specific reasons other than the general ones already mentioned why a Christian communicator may have low credibility. In some cases it is because the communicator is a new, inexperienced convert to Christ. He may lack a so-called "good" background or have no other basis for his authority than his experience with Christ. Many mature Christians view the "Jesus people" in this light. Therefore they may have little confidence in the basic conversion experience of these different people. The Scriptures give examples of Jesus teaching the disciples to guard against making judgments about people who had recently accepted Christ's teachings but had different life-styles in some areas than the disciples.

Moses suffered from this type of credibility loss. He showed his inexperience and lack of knowledge of God's plan for His people by losing his temper, trying to identify with his oppressed people by an act of violence. Bridging the gap from the king's palace, where he had grown up, to the slaves' quarters had to be done another way—God's way. Later God gave him the credibility he needed to be accepted by the Israelites as their leader. God gave him the experience needed for him to be credible and the power to prove to his people that God had really called him to lead them out of Egypt.

Some Christian messengers fail to achieve credibility with the people to whom they want to minister because they lack *cultural empathy*. This term is frequently used in government textbooks for civil servants going overseas to represent their government. It is a term that ought really to be understood by any sincere witness of God's truth. Any manifestation of cultural superiority, especially in speech, is apt to be resented by the people to whom we try to minister.

Communication channels are often clogged by improper use of language. People who act as if their culture is superior to the culture of the people to whom they minister will experience a credibility gap of significant proportion, seriously hindering their efforts to communicate. The important thing is to recognize that each culture has different features from other cultures. Communication has to be adjusted accordingly and exercised in an attitude of understanding of the people's cultural differences and attitudes. This would be also true in the experience of a Christian brought up in a sheltered home trying to communicate with persons reared in a ghetto.

Inconsistency is another cause for loss of credibility. A person who says one thing and practices a life-style completely contrary to or out of harmony with his message will not be believed. The "now" generation with its emphasis on "tell it as it is" is quite adept at seeing through "phonies." In Titus 1:6 we read that an elder or responsible leader in the church must show his right to be believed and to be accepted as a leader by ruling his own household, disciplining his children in love. This means that he must show the people with whom he is communicating God's Word that his life-style or manner of living is consistent with his message.

Indecisiveness is another reason why some Christian communicators are not believed. They seem unsure of the truth of what they are saying, as if they did not know by their own experiences that God's Word is true. They are what we call "wishy-washy," trying to please everyone, offending no one, and failing to take a stand on issues when necessary. They are afraid of the consequences of speaking the truth without fear and favor. They fail to see that children, who seem to have "antennae" especially tuned in to what is true and what isn't, often lose respect for them. Children who have a healthy outlook on life usually tell us what they think; they are not inhibited as adults are by the "what will he think of me" or "what will this cost me" syndrome in their decision-making. Perhaps this is one reason why Jesus used a little child as an object lesson for His disciples. He wanted them to learn to be decisive in their character, not afraid to take a stand for the right, believing God to take care of the consequences. Peter finally learned this lesson on the Day of Pentecost, but occasionally he found it difficult to practice it, especially in the area of racial relations and cultural differences (see Galatians 2:14). Indecisiveness can easily affect our credibility.

Unpreparedness to declare God's Word can also affect the credibility of teachers. If we do not know the Word of God well because we have failed to spend time in preparation, including listening to God and to our class members, we shall be unsuccessful in communicating the message. The lack of preparation makes us not only suspect because of our lack of knowledge in content, but also in personal relationships. We can turn off people because of this deficiency. The presentation lacks authority and influence because it lacks a necessary ingredient to make it credible to the audience.

Overdependence on experience to the neglect of the basic doctrines of the Christian Church can also be a part of this unpreparedness. The message that lacks foundation in God's truth has little credibility. It becomes man's message instead of God's declaration.

Remedies and Suggestions

As messengers of God who desire to communicate to this troubled world God's cosmic plan, including His pronouncements on moral and spiritual sins and His way of salvation for man through Christ, we can be credible witnesses of God. How?

We develop experience quickly as we pray and study God's Word. Security results because we are assured of God's being our ever-present help in time of need! Perhaps God will assure us in some unusual manner as He did Moses by the burning bush. Moses no doubt often recalled the experience when he was tempted to lose confidence in his divine call. It helped him to renew his faith in God's ultimate purpose for His people to bring them into the Promised Land. Moses' renewed credibility in God, based on actual experience, gave him confidence to undertake the great task God had given him. God then was able to give him credibility with the Israelites so that they eventually accepted Moses as their divinely appointed leader for the great Exodus from Egypt to Canaan.

As we gain experience by practice God will give us greater credibility. God showed by signs and wonders, which He did through His servant Moses, that He had indeed called this former prince, the protégé of Pharaoh's daughter, this murderer who had tried by violence to show his anger against his people's oppressors, the Egyptians. Moses had indeed learned a great deal about God and the need for patience during his 40 years of exile in the wilderness. Moses let God do His work in His way, showing that he was indeed a Jew, not an Egyptian, and that he had been destined to lead his people out of bondage into freedom.

The 10 plagues culminating with the Passover event

established Moses' credibility, so that this great host of people was willing to follow him on his way to the Promised Land. The miraculous Red Sea crossing and final escape from the wicked Pharaoh so united the people behind Moses that he was able to lead them on toward Sinai and the establishment of a nation called Israel. This entire experience seems incredible, but it is indeed one of the great historical events showing the intervention of God. It changed an impulsive, mixed-up young man into a dynamic leader of God's chosen people.

The early Christians, many of whom lacked formal education, experienced the power of God working through them, confirming the preaching of Christ as the Messiah. Jesus said that signs of authority to give credulity to the message would be forthcoming. Miracles of healing, deliverance from demon possession, gifts of expression, and marvelous signs of supernatural preservation from harm would attest to the divine authority of the early Christian believers. All of these experiences became reality after Pentecost when the early believers received the baptism of the Holy Spirit and fire. Cultural gaps were also bridged, just as we see happen today when Christ's servants are faithful in believing this promise of Mark 16: 17, 18.

Christ's messengers can achieve cultural empathy as they study the customs, language, and attitudes of the people to whom they seek to communicate God's message. This takes serious study, application, and prayer. It means taking time to sit with people and talk with them, listening to their ideas and concerns. It means overcoming any cultural or intellectual arrogance and learning to appreciate other cultures, including the subculture of the American ghettos. As we become better informed and consequently more understanding of the differences between the cultures of the communicator and the listener, we are able by the help of the Holy Spirit to overcome cultural gaps.

Inconsistency can only be dealt with by a willingness to expose oneself to the scrutiny of God's Word. The Holy Spirit reveals clearly what the problems are. Then the individual can sincerely commit them to Christ, asking for forgiveness and making restitution. For a person to continue to proclaim a message in which he no longer believes and which he therefore doesn't practice is utter folly and detrimental to God's cause. The posture of hypocrisy can be easily acquired by gifted people who begin to rely on their human gifts and techniques of communication instead of relying on the Holy Spirit.

The prevention of such a posture is found in Christian discipline advocated and practiced by the apostle Paul (1 Corinthians 9:15-27). He did not want to become a castaway by his lack of self-discipline after preaching to others. How he handled the problem of cultural differences in communication is also explained in these verses. Study these verses carefully, reading them in different translations to clarify the great truths that Paul had been taught by God about credibility.

People who lack spiritual fortitude to make decisions that may be unpopular can overcome this failure by taking time to consider God's will about these fears, asking for specific Scriptures to fortify their faith, and then deliberately doing what they know has to be done, trusting God to take care of the consequences. This same policy needs to be applied by parents and teachers especially because we are surrounded by a culture of permissiveness in the training of children. Today as never before we need parents, teachers, and other leaders who possess the spiritual fortitude to stand for God-given convictions and to win the confidence of the persons for whom they are responsible before God.

Anyone who wants to communicate effectively for God must prepare his presentations adequately by building a strong foundation of knowledge of God's truth as found in His Word. This involves taking time for careful, consistent study. Evidence of truth should be well documented in order that the intellectual man will accept it. Dr. Francis Schaeffer has been especially used in this area to help many confused intellectuals discover that God really is "the rewarder of them who diligently seek Him." It took many years of preparation and even now involves consistent study in order for him to have credibility in the eyes of these seeking persons who have to perceive truth in a rational manner. It is at this point especially where dependence on the spiritual power of revelation is necessary to apply the truth of God's Holy Word to these inquiring souls.

After the communicator has done all that he can to establish rapport with his hearers by securing his credibility within limits, he has to depend on the Holy Spirit to apply the truth, convincing one of sin and shortcoming in God's sight, looking at one's actions in the light of God's scrutiny, and believing that only through Christ can one be made righteous in God's sight. The Holy Spirit's work is to establish the credibility of the *message*, as well as to confirm the faith of the believing communicator that the "gospel is the power of God unto salvation."

Summary

The credibility gap that exists today between social classes, races, generations, leaders, and people has caused many to "tune out" any message delivered by someone who does not agree with their way of thinking. In Christian communications this problem can be solved. First, one must recognize when credibility is assisting in transmitting and receiving the message. If signs of incredibility appear, one must consider the reasons for the deficiency. Second, if the cause can be remedied because it originates in the communicator (teacher, parent, etc.) himself, then steps should be taken to do so. Finally, the results have to be left in the hands of God, who has specifically stated that the Holy Spirit will confirm the declaration of His Word to the sincere seeker of truth.

Christ was an example to us who desire to communicate His plan, His way to needy people. He commenced His ministry under the anointing of the Holy Spirit, being well prepared to communicate God's message. He knew the truth, practiced it in His daily living, empathized with all types of people with whom He communicated. His life-style was consistent with His teaching. He spoke with authority and decisiveness as a true prophet of God. He always directed His hearers' attention to God's Word as the truth through which true liberty can be experienced and as the criterion by which all men will be judged. We must follow His example if we truly want to be credible communicators of God's truth in our day.

Although secular men depend on natural charisma to persuade people of their credibility, Christians must depend on God to confirm His Word by supernatural charisma and to overcome the extreme skepticism and fragmentation of our society by His Spirit. Above all, we must always remember that the distinguishing mark of Christ's followers, giving them credibility in the eyes of those who would believe, is their love one for the other (see John 13:35).

6 : Improving Listening Skills

The teacher or person transmitting the message can control the input of knowledge to his students or receivers of the message. Therefore emphasis is placed in the science of communications on improving the quality of transmission; however, not as much thought has been given to the *receiver* of the message. Christian educators have thought more in terms of developing excellence in speaking on the part of the teacher, and placing great value upon the ability to articulate one's ideas and knowledge. As a result, the skill of listening has often been forgotten.

Jesus placed great emphasis on the skill of listening. He encouraged active listening that involved the receiver in thinking about the ideas He was presenting. He also encouraged people to put into practice what He was saying. He promised that by doing so their understanding of what He was teaching would increase.

Frequently in the Old Testament God spoke through the prophets calling on His people to listen to Him. Often He denounced Israel's deafness and dullness of heart, a spiritual perceptual handicap which caused them to follow their own way, rejecting His warnings. Because of their inattentiveness and inadequate listening ability, God rated them as poor students and slow in grasping spiritual truths. These people lacked understanding of God's revelation of His will and purpose for their lives largely because they did not *want* to listen to God's messengers. Their mind-set, in other words, prohibited them from hearing what God was trying to say to them through His messengers. On the other hand, there are some hearers or students who do *not know how* to listen. They have not trained their minds to retain spoken data. Basis concepts, which others in the class or audience have retained well, are often not recalled by at least 50 percent of the audience.

A Christian communicator needs then to improve the quality of his output or expression so that the receivers will understand and retain the message better. He needs to try to avoid as much as possible interference to the transmission of the message and its reception. He must pay more attention to the receivers and train them to listen better. The input of the receiver of a communication is more apt to be conceptualized by him, thought given to its implications in terms of his past experiences, and some positive action taken if he is trained in the skill of listening.

Improving listening skills of students in our classes or of people in our audiences could mean a tremendous upgrading of spiritual knowledge. By greater receptivity to learning Christian truth as it is transmitted through the auditory channels of hearers, the new knowledge is more likely to become integrated in the hearers' minds, contemplated, and remembered.

It seems logical to assume also that as the Holy Spirit uses this knowledge to bring spiritual enlightenment to the receivers, more lives will be changed for God's glory and more effective action taken, not only in the receiver's personal life, but also in the lives of others with whom he shares what he has learned of God's truth. Teacher and students need to work together to improve the quantity and quality of listening.

Improving the Quality of Reception

The effective communicator develops the art of listening himself to the ones whom he seeks to instruct or to persuade. He recognizes that communication is not only a language process but a people process. The significance of becoming a person involved in personalized, qualitative communication intrigues him more than the lure of mass communication.

The skilled communicator knows the importance of using as the medium of expression of his ideas a language that is readily understood by the hearers. This involves the use of what is called by Dennett the explanatory or descriptive level of speaking or writing. It is the level which Jesus used most effectively, appealing to the hearer's reason and logic, relating new divine truths to past experiences of His listeners. Sometimes He used the language of the heart appeal, speaking at the emotional level of language. In individual conversations with intellectuals like religious rulers He expressed profound truths in intellectual terms, involving the higher and more creative level of reasoning. Even when He was a boy 12 years of age He must have used this level in discussing spiritual truths with church leaders at the temple. At an early age Jesus demonstrated His superior knowledge of communication by "sitting in the midst of the doctors [teachers of the Law of Moses], both hearing them [listening] and asking them questions [a wide-awake, interrogative student]" (see Luke 2:46). Apparently some of His questions stumped the professors for we read that "all that heard him were astonished at his understanding and answers" (v. 47). The inference seems to be that on this occasion He used the intellectual level of language to which these learned men would listen and respond.

Teachers improve the degree of listening efficiency of their students as they prepare or make ready the minds of the students for understanding the lesson. A misleading assumption, commonly held by the teaching profession and other professions involved in communication, is that listening ability depends largely on intelligence. By overly exaggerating the importance of intelligence in the development of listening skill, we have commited two serious errors. First, we are inferring that people who do not listen well are not intelligent enough to understand what we are saying (we may be expressing ourselves poorly, using the wrong vocabulary or incorrect level of language for them). Second, we are overlooking the fact that listening is a skill, and not all intelligent persons have acquired this skill through training or experience. Some acquired it early in their academic careers but lost it as they grew older for a variety of reasons. The facts presented by research show that poor listening skills can be exhibited by persons of low to high intelligence. My own experience with students supports these conclusions.

What is lacking? Many teachers seem to expose students to new concepts without carefully introducing them to the key words (several of which may be totally unfamiliar to the listeners) and making sure that they understand the meanings of these words in the *context* in which they are to be used in the lesson. Often Bible verses are memorized by students before they understand the meanings of the key words. Bible stories can be stored as unassociated data in a child's mind. Later he may make strange interpretations of the meaning of the story simply because the storyteller did not properly prepare him to understand the context in which the story occurred.

The pupils and other listeners who are adequately introduced to a presentation involving unfamiliar concepts usually will approach the learning task with confidence and interest. Launching into communications which the teacher knows are difficult to understand should always be preceded by readiness instruction, focusing on key words and concepts.

An example of this would be the study of the doctrine of justification, which was one of the key teachings of the Protestant Reformation. If a teacher were introducing this study to a class of modern-day teen-agers by asking the meaning of the key word "justification," he would probably find that no one could really define the term. In asking what "justify" meant, he probably would receive the modern meaning of "excusing oneself, making an alibi for a wrongdoing." This meaning, of course, would be completely misleading to the class in attempting to understand what God means by justification, and as the apostle Paul used the term when writing to the church at Rome (Romans 4, 5). On the other hand, if the word here defined in terms the teen-agers could understand, such as the act of eradicating (wiping out on the police records the account of a crime which a person had really committed) they would understand it. Basic concepts such as the seriousness of the crime, the fairness of the verdict of guilty, the imposed penalty's appropriateness to the seriousness of the crime, would need to be emphasized. The guilty person knows that there is no hope, no way of escape in the natural. Then someone with great influence says, "I will not only pardon you for this crime, but I will destroy the record of it; you will be free not only from the guilt and the penalty but also the record of the deed. You will live a new life by my power and be just in my sight. If you believe that I paid the penalty for your sins, then I will arrange with God to destroy the record of your sins from His book and you shall live just as if you had never sinned!"

Think of how many questions this brief introduction to the word "justification" could stimulate in thinking teen-agers' minds today. Then you may realize that an awareness of the need for readiness to learn is an important key to listening.

Another way to improve the reception of a message is to relate the communication to the needs of the students. Jesus, as we have previously studied, always did this in His teaching. Today we must understand the general impatience of youth, their impulsivity, their desire for immediate action, their expectation of instant solutions to problems. A wise teacher recognizes these tendencies, accommodates to them, but does not compromise Jesus' message. After he has secured the attention of the students and expresses an understanding of their frustration, he can then get them to think of all facets of the question, "telling it as it is," not only as they see it at the moment, but how others see it who have been looking at the problem for a long time. After studying God's Word to learn what He has to say on the subject, then encourage prayer for guidance. If there is some course of action that your students can take to alleviate the problem in the area in which they live, they should be encouraged to think of how they can legitimately help within the framework of the Christian ethic. The impatience and enthusiasm of young people can be effectively channeled into avenues of blessings to others, if they are helped to listen to understanding adults who know how to make truths relate to their needs and problems.

Also students can be helped to listen better if distractions are controlled as much as possible. Extraneous noise and visual stimuli not related to the topic being discussed have to be removed in order that some easily distracted persons can pay attention and concentrate. If Jimmy is distracted by the bee that has entered the classroom, it will not do much good to say to him, "Never mind the bee, Jimmy. Pay attention to the lesson." Jimmy may be afraid of the bee or he may have a great desire to catch it (without getting stung, of course) and let it fly outdoors to freedom. Jimmy is not going to learn much from the Bible lesson as long as the bee is in the room!

Teachers need to develop informal, relaxed atmospheres for learning in which the students cooperate with the teacher and one another to listen to and to discuss God's message. Such an atmosphere gives students many opportunities to participate in the learning situation, under the skillful guidance of the teacher who structures and controls the environment so that it remains a healthy one.

It is a good idea to vary the auditory input of spiritual truth by using audio aids such as tape recorders and phonographs. When it relates to the lesson it is often beneficial to the class to present a taped message or testimony from some well-known and admired person. This can improve listening tremendously and keep interest high. It helps also to bring in a change of voice and personality by exchanging classes with another teacher or by inviting an outside speaker to discuss an area of interest with them. Stimulation to listen well can be found if we only look for it. The cassette tape recorder has made this form of audio assistance readily accessible to most teachers today.

Defective listening is often caused by defensive actions on the part of the listeners. A tendency to evaluate a speaker by his mannerisms, to judge him prematurely because his opinions disagree with the receiver's often causes poor listening. Recent reports indicate this tendency seems to be increasing today. There seems to be more and more an inclination to shut out by various means (some rather noisy ones such as booing, etc.) the communications of persons who do not for some reason appeal to the listener. While listening, the main objective should be to understand what the speaker is saying, be able to interpret it fairly to others, and then evaluate and make decisions about its value or lack of it.

One major reason for poor listening is that the human brain thinks much faster than we can talk. The receiving speed is greater than the expressive speed. Words race at a fantastic speed through our brains but the average speaking rate of most Americans is around 125 words per minute. The lag between the output speed of the transmitter and the input speed of the receiver is too frustratingly slow for the human brain to process. This is the reason why so many listeners (especially "fast" thinkers) think about something else at the same time. Woolgathering, or legitimate thinking on other important matters not related to the topic being discussed, can be prevented by training one's mind to think beyond what the speaker is saying, to indulge in divergent conceptualizing related to the topic. This keeps the listener's mind actively engaged in thinking about the ideas being presented. Many productive ideas have been generated in active, creative minds by good listening even to dull speeches!

Other people are poor listeners because they try to memorize the details presented by the speaker. This is impossible and leads to a faulty, sketchy understanding of what the speaker has actually said. Students need to be trained to listen for the major ideas and sufficient supporting facts to be able later to judge the validity of what has been said, to draw conclusions from the speaker's presentation, and to be able to ask questions about any obscure points.

Taking notes is usually a very useful aid to listening for

older students. Reception is better when there is involvement beneficial to the receiver. Some people do not express themselves well in writing and will find note-taking a distraction rather than an aid to listening. However, most people find that expressing the major ideas and supporting details of a speech or lecture in writing deepens the impression on their minds of what the communicator is actually discussing. This involves the listener in the preliminary selecting and organizing of the ideas presented. If note-taking is not done in this manner, but is considered as a dictation activity, the results will be minimal. It would be better for that person to tape-record a lesson, replay it, and teach himself to take selective notes on the lecture in a quiet place.

The principal ingredient of good listening to God's truth is openness of our minds to the thoughts as they are presented. If we listen with prejudice, defensiveness, fear, anxiety, or an obsession to discount the speaker because we don't want to receive God's message, then we shall continue to be poor listeners or even become "deaf" to certain areas of God's Word.

An openness, on the other hand, does not mean being gullible and not discriminating between what is really truth, verified by God's Word, and what is man's opinion. It does mean that the Holy Spirit is able to guide the open-minded listener into genuine understanding of God's truths. Luke 24:45 explains this experience in the lives of some of Christ's disciples after the Resurrection.

A teacher or other communicator of the gospel of Jesus Christ can do much with the help of the Holy Spirit to dispel the fear some people have of really listening to God's truths. By seeking to create an atmosphere of trust and support through honest and open interaction with others, the communicator discovers that more learning takes place because the people, including the teacher, have learned to listen to one another and above all to God.

Listen and Think

The teacher can help to set a purpose for listening so that the students understand what they are supposed to learn from listening. This can be done by asking some important lead-in questions that start the listeners to think. Jesus captured the attention of His disciples one day to a very crucial issue by asking a question, "Whom do men say that I am?" This was a news lead-in, a public opinion poll of a type to attract the disciples' attention and to stimulate their thinking about the more important question, "Whom do *you* say that I am?"

Listeners can be encouraged to think by showing them how to listen to key words, major ideas, and significant details. This helps them to avoid the problem of cluttering their minds with many details, attempting to "tape-record" verbatim in their minds what the speaker said. First, instruct them how to do this by using a short, well-organized speech or sermon (use a tape or record for this activity), stopping at natural intervals in the speech to question the class and ask them for the key words which they have identified because of their frequent repetition in use or meaning (synonyms). Then ask them when one section of the speech has been played what the major points presented were. Here one must be careful to involve the poorer listeners as much as possible in the step-by-step procedure. Often teen-agers and adults will surprise you how easily they will grasp ideas when they are given hints on how to listen well for word signals and clues. The next step would be to ask the students to apply the same principles to listening to the lesson for the day.

Encouraging students to ask questions, to infer meanings from what they have heard, to think about the implications of Christian truth to their own lives will stimulate listening and thinking. Thoughts of this type are more apt to result in action. The listener has become an involved one. The effects on his own personal life of this thoughtful assimilation of divine truth to his own experiences will be noticeable because the Holy Spirit has a base of understood gospel truth on which to work in his heart and life.

Provide time for responses that are more than mechanical feedbacks. The quality of the response from learners should gradually increase as children become older and reach the stage for serious thinking in their development. This can be aided by giving more thought to lead-in as well as follow-up questions. Most children by the time they are eight can tell you more about a Bible story than the *who, what, when, where* type of factual knowledge. Important concepts of scriptural truth can be taught and understood when properly illustrated and introduced. Listening skills of all children should be continuously strengthened by teaching them to think as well as listen.

One is, of course, aware that great differences in thinking ability exist in any random sample of human beings. But the fact remains that the minds of many would-be followers of Christ need stretching. Jesus certainly taught all types of people to listen and to think. He didn't say to Peter, "You come from a fishing village and don't know much about theology or sophisticated truths, so I don't expect you to learn much about God's plan or His truths as I teach them. After all we only have three years, Peter, and your background is *so limited.*" Of course Jesus did not say or even imply this poor expectancy of Peter's ability. He believed that some day Peter would become the leading apostle of the Christian Church, teaching the gospel of Jesus Christ with power, eloquence, and knowledge.

As teachers, we must ask God to show us what the expectancy level of understanding is for each of our students. If we ourselves label them, we shall excuse ourselves for failure to teach them.

Summary

Everyone needs to learn to listen well in order to receive, with understanding and retention communications through the auditory channel. The skill of listening starts with the young child and should continue to be developed throughout one's life by instruction and practice, as so much time is spent in this activity.

Jesus emphasized the value of being good listeners. He was aware of the fact that communication is a process of people, involving living receivers, as well as a process of language, involving a code and different levels of language understanding.

Jesus placed emphasis on the responsibility of the hearer as well as the teacher to develop an atmosphere in which learning through listening to the communicator and to other learners could function in trust and confidence. Many of the so-called modern techniques for improving listening were practiced by Christ also. He demonstrated to us, who seek to teach others, the importance of attracting attention to a subject by a well-chosen lead-in question, controlling distractions (such as a sick man being lowered through the ceiling of His classroom, Mark 2:2-4), and dealing with the emotional causes of poor listening, including defensiveness and prejudice.

Let us also learn from Jesus' example. Through wise applications of good teaching techniques let us instruct our students in the skill of listening. As we develop the trained ear among our listeners, teaching them to think when they listen, they will be more responsive to the transmitted message applied to their hearts by the Holy Spirit.

7 : Improving Students' Reading Skills

Throughout the world today ability to read is a sign of being educated at least to the level of being able to function adequately in a literate society. Underdeveloped nations strive to raise the percentage of people in their respective countries who can read. They believe that literacy opens doors to the intellectual and economic growth of their citizens.

Wherever missionaries of Jesus Christ have gone they have often been involved in some form of literacy work. In many countries of the world, missionaries have not only taught people to read; they have often had first to devise a code or alphabet in which the sounds of the native language could be transcribed. This meant also that portions of the Bible had first to be translated into this new code. Then someone had to teach key people in the area in which this code was spoken to decode the printed portion of the Bible. It was at that time that the mysterious experience of "making a book talk to you," reading the Word of God in one's own native language, began for these primitive people. They had never known that their highly developed spoken language could be put into signs and symbols (a code) which could be learned and read with understanding.

Schools were opened to spread literacy throughout an area where the newly written language was spoken. Eventually a trained, literate group of born-again believers emerged and formed the nucleus of the Christian Church in that section of God's harvest field. As literacy increases, the demand for literature intensifies. Distributing Christian literature is today one of the most important ways of transmitting God's message to non-Christians, of training Christians to assume responsibility for the developing of the Christian Church in their lands.

In spite of all the Christian literature available in many different languages today, the work of making the revelation of God in Christ known through the printed page is far from accomplished. Christians need also to know how to read with selection and discrimination. We need to teach Christians how to read and provide them with a Bible in their own language. We must tell them of the forces at work in the world today which seek to use this newfound literacy to expose them to all kinds of propaganda in an attempt to capture their minds. World Communists especially have boasted for years that they would let the missionary teach the people to read, but they would provide attractively printed literature for them to read. The output of this type of literature is so tremendous throughout the world, it is impossible to estimate how much damage has been done to the minds and lives of many new literates who have not been taught how to discriminate between good and evil in what they read. Unfortunately many of these people have thought that anything printed must be sacred and therefore accepted as truth.

Christian Literacy and American Youth

Many young people in the Western World are ignorant of God's Word. Although Bibles are plentiful in America, many of them are not read. Because many leaders in established churches have attacked the Bible, refused to accept it as the Word of God, many Western World homes have not fostered the habit of reading or studying the Bible. In fact, the TV screen now provides the principal means of communication in many American homes.

In the search for reality, deluded young people, looking for mystical experiences or highs as they call it, are experimenting with drugs whereby they attempt to escape the dreary mundaneness of their natural lives. As primitive peoples have done for centuries, they are seeking a religious experience, a new way of knowing through "mind-blowing" drugs. Satan has thus further deluded some into following a cult which ultimately leads many of its adherents to sell their souls to him and to worship the occult. Through neglect of or disbelief in God's Word they have allowed their minds to be deceived by Satan.

A contrasting movement is, however, sweeping across the nation. It too is a movement primarily of the young. They have opened their minds to Jesus' claims and have decided to turn from the nothingness of the world of drugs, sex, the occult, or from the disillusionment of humanism to the Word of God. Many of these people have been delivered from their dependency on drugs and alcohol and have found that Christ is the answer to the sin problem of their lives. They now are lovers of the Bible, read and study it with great devotion, trying to make up for the gross spiritual ignorance of their childhood.

The question that Philip, the Jerusalem deacon, asked an Ethiopian official on his way home from Jerusalem is still very valid today. It is an important question, whether we are addressing it to persons who have been exposed to daily reading of the Bible in their homes, to new literates who are reading it for the first time in their own language, or for the "Jesus people" who feel that they have been cheated of their spiritual heritage by adults and their ignorance of God's Word. The question addressed to an educated politician as he read from the prophet Isaiah, was simply, "Do you understand what you are reading?" This learned man acknowledged that he did not understand about whom Isaiah was writing (Isaiah 53). So Philip introduced this African administrator to Jesus Christ, the Messiah (see Acts 8).

How can we as communicators of the revelation of Jesus Christ help people to read the Bible and also to understand the meaning of what they read?

Improving Visual Input

We have discussed the importance of the auditory input and emphasized that much knowledge, not only of the world around us, but also of spiritual truths as revealed to the mind, comes to us through the channel of listening. This is a rather slow way of processing data, we know, because the reception is slowed to about 125 words per minute by the limitations of speaking the code. One can learn to read much more rapidly, be more selective in what he reads, and can acquire much more information and knowledge by reading than any other form of input. This is true, of course, only if one knows how to read well.

Teachers in church schools are often surprised that so many of their students are poor readers. The high rate of problem readers (at least 25 percent of the present school population, according to the latest U.S. Government estimate) should concern Christian educators. A great majority of juvenile delinquents, adolescents with mental health problems, unemployed persons, and school dropouts have severe reading disabilities. This is true not only in the United States but in other countries as well.

Above all, ignorance of the Bible, even among our children and adolescents who are good readers, is a situation that needs serious consideration. Let us determine at least to open our eyes to the need and try by God's grace to do something about it.

We can now provide the Bible in a language that is comprehensible to the literate young person. There is much reading material available that presents Biblical truths so that young people can understand them. The Bible translation *Good News for Modern Man* is especially helpful to the "now" generation and is read with interest by many people who are experiencing Bible reading for the first time. It can provide a fresh overview also for many Christians who are already familiar with the King James translation.

Another way to improve our students' reading skills is to provide interesting and attractive reading material for them. This material should invite readers to enjoy it and present gospel truth conforming to the Scriptures. Colorful cartoons and comics often attract immature readers especially who benefit from picture clues that aid them in reading the code.

Knowing Reading Levels

A teacher should know the reading level of each one of his students, adults as well as children. You, as his teacher, should guide the student to select titles that interest him because of their subject matter or content and are enjoyable to him because they are written at the level of his reading vocabulary.

You should make a quick check of whether or not the instructional material used in Sunday school for your class is readable for every member. For young adults and older persons, assign them to read silently one section of the quarterly containing about 400 words. As soon as they have finished reading, give each one a sheet of paper on which you have listed 10 questions based on the section. Each student should try to answer the questions without referring to the text. The goal would be to answer correctly at least seven of the 10 questions. The questions should involve more than just factual responses. One question should be based on the major thought emphasized in the section. About five questions could involve factual recall, and the others should demand a higher level of thinking, including logical inferences and conclusions. After the answer papers have been handed in, go over the answers to the questions orally, asking different members in the class to respond. Give them guidance for their future studying and reading the lesson, informing the class that this initial testing was only a trial run. Give some hints for better reading. Class members should contribute to this activity.

This challenge can be interesting to your class and not embarrassing if everyone is encouraged to participate and, if they choose to do so, work with a partner on the questions. The next week a similar trial run can be made. Ask for pupils to indicate whether or not they did a better job on the second trial. Correct these orally in class, each team correcting his own. Goals should be set before the next reading. A goal might be simply trying to reach the 70 percent comprehension goal set for the first week. For others it may mean a higher score than last week reading a 400-word selection, faster than they did previously, but achieving at least 70 percent comprehension. The same procedure for correction and teamwork can be used.

On the third week everyone should be ready, except the poor readers or nonreaders, for the final test in reading. In preparation for this test, read the questions to them *before* they start reading. Then let them read and answer the questions on a written sheet of paper as before, handing their papers in for checking. Anyone who does not want to take the test should not be required to do so. By the time the third week's activity is finished, you should know which students should be encouraged to study their lesson with someone else and who can read the material with at least 70 percent comprehension. The good readers who were rather poor on their recall in the first trial should have improved their skill in this area considerably by the simple techniques of setting specific purposes for reading and previewing the questions before they read; then reading attentively and answering the questions from memory.

This simple exercise might be a jolt to some adults who have allowed themselves to lose considerable reading skill since their school years. They need to be shown that they can train their brain to take in ideas through the visual stimuli and to organize the ideas in a way that helps them to recall with only *one* reading the important ideas which they have received visually.

The importance of this type of activity will be realized by the students and teacher alike when they begin to recognize an increase in retained knowledge of the Word of God and improved understanding of concepts which previously have eluded them. Any skill needs consistent training through instruction and practice. Reading is one skill that should not be neglected but should become a lifetime habit.

I have known Congolese adults who learned to read late in life. One would call them semiliterates, but they became very good students of the Bible through daily reading practice and assistance from younger readers. Motivation to learn more about God through the Scriptures caused them to improve their reading ability to the literacy level needed for reading the Bible with understanding. Many teachers in America agree that lack of motivation to learn to read well is one of the major reasons for inefficient reading by many persons in highly industrialized societies such as the United States and Britain.

Prevention Is Better than Cure

It is now widely accepted by many educators that the problem of developing good adult readers, who can adequately acquire through the visual channel important information and knowledge to benefit them in all areas of their lives, can best be resolved by concentrating on preventing reading failure in our children and teen-agers. As Christians involved in communicating with our students, expecting many of them to be able to read the study materials, Sunday school literature, as well as helpful books from the church library, we should take time to find out how well they can read.

It is quite simple to find out whether or not a child or adolescent can read the Christian education materials you are using in your school. When a child brings a book from the library, parents can use the same procedure to learn whether or not the book is too easy or too difficult for him. Select a section of the material of about 200 words. Ask the child or adolescent to read orally to you. Jot down all key words he mispronounces or omits. If he hesitates for several seconds at an unfamiliar word, pronounce it for him and count it as an error. Then ask him five questions on the selection, one of which requires him to express the main idea of the 200-word selection. He should be able to answer at least *four* of the *five* questions, showing that he did understand and recall well what he read. For material that he is going to read on his own without assistance in pronouncing the key words, he should, in the oral reading, not make more than *three* different pronunciation errors in 100 words. When use is made of teacher-directed material for which assistance is given in identifying the key words in both pronunciation and meaning, not more than *five* of these words should be mispronounced in the oral reading testing.

Identifying and Helping Poor Readers

Difficult material will frustrate poor readers and it will be a complete waste of time for them to try to read it. They will feel that "it is Greek to them," and often refuse to read or study reading material that is above their reading level. For such readers in your class, try to find easier material for them to read which covers the same topics. A Bible paraphrase that is easy to read is Taylor's *The Living Bible*. If this is not available, arrange for the child to work with a good reader as a partner.

One of the most beneficial aids to any class is for the teacher to take a few minutes at the beginning of each class to discuss key words of the lesson, writing each word on the board and beside it writing the word in easy code. Students themselves will be able to pronounce the word without the teacher's help. Discuss the meaning of each word in the context in which it is used in the Bible exposition. It is important that the teacher try by skillful questioning to have the students (ask the poorer readers to pronounce the words) discover for themselves how to pronounce and to understand each unfamiliar key word.

Teachers note today that the spoken vocabulary of many children and adolescents is different from the reading vocabulary of study-type materials. This is primarily a result of increased television viewing. Therefore, a guided exposure to the vocabulary before reading materials in which new concepts are presented will be of great help to most students. We must remember that much of the Biblical vocabulary that we use today is often very unfamiliar to the uninitiated ears of many children who have seldom had the Bible read to them. Other children have memorized Biblical vocabulary but have only vague ideas about its actual meaning.

Problem readers should be identified by the Christian

communicator but should not be embarrassed by being asked to read orally in a group situation. A good way to learn about the reading abilities of each class member above 8 years of age is to ask for volunteers to read various portions of the lesson while the *others listen*. Usually only good readers will offer to do so. After the reading, ask the child or adolescent to tell the class briefly what he read, interpreting the thought in his own words. Ask the class to question him on any other ideas he did not mention. Make note of any evidences of reading difficulty in your mind. At the same time keep the attention of the class focused on the major ideas of the lesson. This will mean that the time is being utilized properly for learning scriptural truths but, at the same time, you are gathering information about the abilities of your students to read with understanding.

Students who do not volunteer to read orally before the class should be tested individually in a quiet corner, using the method explained earlier. This can be done while the other students are doing the handwork or written application of the lesson. Some teachers may plan to do this in a private conference.

Genuine interest in improving your students' reading skills will be appreciated by all students except the ones who are very defensive about their handicap. These students often need professional help beyond the capability of a Christian education teacher to give. However, often these students, who find it difficult to learn through the visual modality because of visual perceptual difficulty in the brain, need auditory clues to help them associate the sound with the symbol and the symbol with the sound. Some children, for example, perceive visually the the letters *sh* but pronounce (decode) them as a *ch* sound. Thus they would see the word *shilling* (symbol for an English coin) and pronounce it *chilling*, which has a very different meaning. These children need to be taught the phonics of the English language sufficiently so that they not only hear the difference between the *sh* and *ch* sounds but see the difference in the letter combinations.

If the Christian teacher can learn that children who are not good readers often are not limited in intelligence (a popular belief now thoroughly discounted by research), but rather find learning by visual memory very difficult, they will be able to find ways to help them in addition to what the school is doing for them.

Churches, especially in the deprived areas of our country, could help considerably by providing after-school tutorial services using Christian volunteers. Many churches can initiate this type of program very successfully, provided that they have the services of a competent Christian educator to coordinate the program, to recruit staff, to develop a programmed form of in-service training for the tutors, and then to integrate the program into the Christian education services of the church.

The major goal of this type of community service should be to honor Christ by helping people not only to find Him as their personal Saviour, but to develop their abilities to function effectively in this world. Reading provides not only a tool for growing in the knowledge of spiritual truth but also for developing the potential that God has given us.

Remembering What We Read

Material read should be meaningful to the receiver. The sooner the ideas are applied to an immediate situation, the better they will be remembered. The Ethiopian official was asked by Philip to believe on Christ after he not only understood the passage in Isaiah which he had been reading, but also other Scriptures related to the gospel as well. Belief followed understanding, and then baptism in water followed belief, showing that he really meant his confession of faith in Christ. Without a doubt, the man never forgot what he learned that day.

Tradition tells us that this new convert brought the gospel to Ethiopia. What a quick learner he was! He must have had a good teacher too, to be able to explain the gospel so well in such a short time. Think also how beneficial it was for this Ethiopian to be able to read the Old Testament Scriptures, especially the ones explained by Philip. He was able to win many souls to Christ in his homeland as he brought the gospel of Jesus to Africa.

If a reader understands the major ideas of what he reads (there is usually one main idea in each paragraph) and perceives as he reads how the important details support the main idea, he will remember better what he reads. The same type of selectivity, organizing of ideas, associating the new with what the person already knows and thinking while one reads, which the good listener does, should be done even more effectively by the reader.

Reading can become a very personalized form of communication, if the reader becomes absorbed in the author's ideas. He must also learn to conceptualize these ideas so well that he can interpret what the author said to some other person. Also the reading act becomes highly personalized when the truth, for example, from the Bible is applied to one's individual life. Action is taken on the thoughts or facts presented as the Ethiopian eunuch did.

As teachers, we should expect decisive actions to result from reading God's Word. Millions of souls have come to know Christ through this medium of communication. Let us then try to develop this skill in our students and also stimulate them to read other good material. A course on how to read and study the Bible would be an excellent one to make available for young people and adults.

Summary

In order to understand what we read, we need to know how to read, what to look for when we read, how to bring all of our attention to the reading task, to set a purpose for reading, to look for key words and ideas, and to organize in meaningful associations the major ideas presented. We must think beyond the author's ideas, applying the basic concepts to our own personal needs and lives.

Learning to read should eventually be the right of every person in this modern day. Many problem readers can be helped by Christians especially, who should not only care about them more than anyone else, but also have some idea *how* to help them. Sometimes this may mean referral to professional persons who specialize in teaching severely disabled readers. At least teachers who want to communicate God's truth should realize how important a person's being able to read with understanding is in the process of communication. As Christian communicators we should encourage Bible reading and serious study of literature that increases one's knowledge of the Bible and Christian living.

One must always remember that the struggle for the minds of men is worldwide today. We should not only be concerned that everyone to whom we are responsible for communicating knows how to read but that he also knows how to discriminate between falsehood and truth. A receptive, trained mind, enlightened by the Holy Spirit, will know the truth and not be deluded by Satan's lies and subtle half-truths.

8 : How to Speak So Others Listen

The apostle Paul reminded Ephesian Christians of their need to communicate with God through prayer (Ephesians 6:18-20). He also requested prayer for himself, that he might be able to speak with boldness, interpreting the gospel of Jesus Christ in such an effective manner that its mystery would be understood by his hearers. There was no doubt that Paul knew his need to communicate effectively with the important persons who were at that time visiting him in the Roman prison. Even though he was in chains, he wanted to communicate the gospel of Jesus Christ boldly and effectively.

How effectively and boldly do we as Christian communicators speak today to the persons whom God brings into the sphere of our influence? We have discussed the problems involved in listening, which are to a great extent the result of present-day living. Most of our young people belong to the TV generation. They have been conditioned to *see* as well as *hear* simultaneously stimuli presented to them. Our teaching, to be effective, needs to be strengthened by presentations involving reception of information through a variety of sensory channels. This will help in transmitting the ideas that God wants communicated to this generation.

However, there are times when speaking becomes the principal means of communication to others even though its limitations are quite obvious because of its dependency on good listening (discussed in chapter 6). Speaking can be effective as a medium of communication, provided that it is not overworked. We need to learn to speak so that others will listen and the Holy Spirit can bring to their attention the major ideas presented. Understanding on the part of the listeners is imperative.

Points to Remember About Speaking

Speaking is a form of expression involving language. Language is symbolic expression, involving the use of symbols called words. According to Everett M. Stowe, it is a mark of humanity as universal as mankind. Language, although diverse in forms, has unity of symbolic function. Man needs to use it wisely to express his emotions and ideas in meaningful symbols to other human beings.

First, an effective speaker must learn to use simple and descriptive words. C. S. Lewis in a speech, "On Moving with the Times," stated that the Christian teacher must be able to translate theology into the language spoken by the people in everyday life. Some teachers try to speak as they would write, using literary language that is intended to be read, not listened to. Lewis points out that many words that we use in Christian teaching are not understood by the uneducated or *differently* educated person.

Lewis further stated that uneducated people are not irrational people. They can follow the explanatory level of language very well, if the ideas presented are communicated in word symbols easily identified by them as related to their experience and interests. Jesus often used the explanatory level of language, appealing to reason and logic, when speaking to uneducated persons. They understood Him because He used simple, descriptive words and other symbols taken from the experiences of the people.

At the same time very profound thoughts can be communicated to people of varied experiential backgrounds when a simple vocabulary is used. A good example of this form of communication is the prologue of the Gospel of John. Deep truths of theology are expressed by John in beautiful, simple words based on language symbols comprehensible to the receivers of the communication.

In illustrating the problem of speaking in word-symbols which have different meanings to people of varied backgrounds, C. S. Lewis presented a word list. One word from this list will suffice to illustrate this point: *Christian*—the word to a secular person expresses approval of someone who is supposed to be unselfish, decent, clean living. On the other hand, this word conveys an entirely different meaning to the regenerated person who uses it in the Biblical sense. A Christian is one who follows Christ's example, who believes in Him as Saviour and Lord, and who practices what he believes by the Holy Spirit dwelling within him. It is very easy today to use word-symbols that convey vastly different meanings to our hearers, many of whom are not familiar with Biblical language.

Second, important ideas should be presented in a variety of ways. Jesus used the imagery of the harvest field and the harvesters, the fish and the fishermen, the servant and the master, the disciple and the teacher to portray the teaching of God about service. Reinforcement of this type of concept is important.

Third, a speaker who wants to be listened to must know his subject and be engrossed in it personally. Many people do not believe the Bible is the Word of God. Starting with the Bible often "turns them off." They have been taught to respect personal experiences, however. The teacher will find that they may listen to personal examples from the experiences of people whom the teacher knows. These testimonies show that faith in Jesus Christ does work. This type of approach can open the way for meaningful dialogue with a searching soul. It can also increase the quality as well as the quantity of listening taking place in an audience situation.

Knowing the subject about which we are speaking means more than an experiential involvement in it. It also means building by daily study and contemplation a background of knowledge which the Holy Spirit can use in communicating a lesson to others. Using expository aids is helpful when elaborating the thoughts God has given you as you study His Word. Then it is time to organize these ideas so that the presentation may solicit continuous attention from the hearers. When they can follow your presentation easily, they listen and learn. An effective speaker knows how to get the attention of his audience at the beginning and how to keep that attention throughout the speech. This means that he knows *what* he is talking about and *how* to talk about it.

Other helpful suggestions would include remembering to be enthusiastic about your subject, believing that God will help you by His Holy Spirit to communicate effectively what is *burning* in your heart. Jeremiah the prophet used these terms to describe the urgency and burden he felt in delivering God's message to Israel. God's messengers need to experience the same type of concern and sense of involvement in the presentation of the gospel.

Younger children learn a great deal through listening if a speaker does not exceed their attention span. It helps to maintain attention if the teacher utilizes the mobility of young children to help in the learning process. Young, squirming children can learn even though in motion, provided that their attention is focused on the learning task. Ask them to come to the chalkboard or flannel board and find a picture represented by a key word in the lesson. Encourage them to act out the story from the Bible lesson. Activities of this type help the active child to maintain attention and learn the spiritual truths being presented. Bible games also can be used effectively to keep the attention of restless children. A two-way type of communication in which the students become involved, reacting by acting out what the teacher has taught them, can also be an effective method of sustaining attention during a lesson presentation.

Communicators need to learn to be themselves in oral expression. Affected speech is distracting to many listeners. Naturalness of speech under the anointing of God attracts people to listen to the *message* and not to be overly preoccupied with the *messenger*. We must avoid focusing the hearers' attention on us as the transmitters of the message. They (the receivers) must focus their attention on the truths presented. Otherwise they will be responding to the human instrument (the communicator or transmitter) rather than responding to Christ, the One whom we are seeking to present and to represent.

Another way to improve speaking is to have a friend evaluate one of your lesson presentations. Expect him to make a candid appraisal of the presentation and to offer suggestions for improvement. A teacher can easily become guilty of "overloading" almost unconsciously, by presenting too many ideas at once so that the audience is not able to grasp them. It could mean also using language that is unintelligible to them because it involves the use of too many unfamiliar words, or too long, complicated sentences. Presenting ideas too rapidly for assimilation by an audience could also result in what psychologists call "overloading." A friend who is perceptive can help you to be aware of this problem.

Dialogue should be encouraged and the danger of

overloading can thus be reduced. Feedback to ideas is important in order to know what points are obscure and have not been clearly understood by the audience. We must train ourselves to "tune in," monitoring our output and the receivers' input as well. Ask for reactions and don't be defensive. Try to find out why the presented ideas have not been thoroughly understood and find the most effective way of remedying the situation. Remember that one is not communicating unless the receiver is understanding the message!

Examples of Effective Speaking

John 4: Jesus' conversation with the Samaritan woman. In this passage, the Lord has given us perhaps the best demonstration of effective communication in the Bible. There were several difficulties encountered which made the communication a challenge to Jesus. It shows God's followers that effective teaching can take place even in adverse circumstances.

The main speaker was tired from a long walk in the hot sun. It was a time for resting, not talking. The object of the communication was a woman, a Samaritan woman, a sinful woman. Several "gaps," as we call them today, existed between the communicator and the student. There was the gap of race, for He was a Jew and she was a Samaritan. She was on the defensive about that gap, feeling inferior and insecure. Then there was the gap of sex; he was a man, she, a woman. The Jews often prayed, "Thank God, I was not born a woman!" Furthermore, the gap of position bothered her (none of these so-called gaps seemed to bother Jesus) for He was a teacher; she, a learner who didn't realize that she had so much to learn about life in one day!

How did Jesus handle this situation? He involved the woman in a dialogue, not a discourse. He started with a meaningful subject, the well and water. He asked for a favor, a drink of water. This immediately made her realize that this Jew was different. He wasn't afraid to communicate to someone from an alien race. He spoke directly and simply about His major concern. He wanted her to know that there was living water for her thirsty soul, that a new way of living could be hers that day by the grace of God.

Jesus handled her distracting questions which showed that she still was listening defensively. But He kept her attention kindly but firmly focused on the subject. The moment of truth arrived when she recognized who Jesus was: He was the Messiah, the One who would explain everything to searching souls like herself! How skillfully Jesus had led her in their dialogue to the place where she understood the truth. Jesus, the Messiah, reached across the many gaps that men had erected and revealed to her that the source of divine life was available to her thirsty soul.

John 9: Jesus communicates on the Light of the World, using a healed blind man as an object lesson. How did Jesus use this blind man's healing to teach an eternal truth? Notice that Jesus taught this truth *before* He healed the blind man, demonstrating the power of God to open eyes blinded both spiritually and physically.

The reactions of the audience were varied. The neighbors of the former blind man were skeptical of his healing. The Pharisees were unwilling to concede that Jesus had healed this man by the power of God. The major truth demonstrated by this miracle, namely, that Jesus is the Light of the World, was not acceptable to them. Fear of the church leaders, who had threatened excommunication to any church members believing on Jesus, paralyzed the healed man's parents so that they refused to commit themselves to the implications of this miracle. Jesus left the former blind man also to witness on his own before the church leaders. He did so fearlessly, with the result that he was the one who benefited the most from this object lesson.

Not only did he testify before the Pharisees to his healing; he also chided them for being so confused in their theology. They were trying to say that God had indeed healed this man but He had used an evil person, an impostor named Jesus, to perform this miracle! This contradictory statement was denounced by the healed man. Later Jesus introduced Himself as the Messiah to him in the temple. Immediately this receptive man believed and worshiped Jesus.

Jesus told him, "I have come into the world to give sight to those who are spiritually blind and to show those *who think they see that they are blind.*" Think how effectively Jesus communicated this truth so that everyone understood it! The disciples learned to focus on major concerns, not controversial issues such as who was to blame for the blind man's condition. This man needed healing, physically and spiritually, not a theological argument! The neighbors, the church leaders, the parents all knew that Jesus was the Light of the World by the time the lesson was completed. Whether they believed this truth or not was their personal responsibility. Jesus had communicated the message so that they understood! The healed man proved to be the best learner of the day by learning experientially what Jesus was teaching.

Acts 2: Peter's discourse on the Day of Pentecost. Peter started with the reactions of the crowd to the coming of the Holy Spirit and the accompanying phenomenon—the miracle of tongues. He quickly dispensed with the opinion that drunkenness was the cause, and called the people's attention to what God had to say to them. In this remarkable discourse, Peter communicated without inhibition what God had put into his heart to say. He showed how this historic outpouring of the Spirit had been prophesied many years previously by Joel, so he used the Scriptures to prove his point that this phenomenon was of God. His audience believed the Scriptures and had great respect for the prophets whose words they heard read every Sabbath in their synagogues. They listened attentively.

Peter spoke of the miracles of expression, of revelation, of judgment which attend the ministry of the Holy Spirit. Then he presented the way of escape from the judgment of God—calling on the name of the Lord, asking for mercy at God's hands. Finally, he proceeded to introduce to them Jesus of Nazareth, the crucified but risen Saviour, the only One on whom they must call in order to be saved. These words were simple but direct; no one could misunderstand what Peter was communicating!

Again Peter turns to the Scriptures to support his claim that Jesus rose from the dead. He quotes David when he prophesied many years before the coming of Christ that the Messiah would be resurrected. Then Peter gives the testimony of all the believers who were witnesses of Jesus' resurrection and ascension. The results of this clear-cut, well-documented, logical and fearless exposition were certainly a proof of the effectiveness of Peter's discourse. The many miracles of conversion that followed proved without doubt that the Holy Spirit had anointed Peter's message and touched the hearts and minds of the listeners to believe the truth.

These model communicators of spiritual truths demonstrated characteristics of effective speaking. They spoke and others listened. Let us as teachers think of these characteristics and apply them with the help of the Holy Spirit.

First, we observe that both Jesus and Peter started

speaking at the point of interest of their respective audiences. These points of interest were the well of water for the Samaritan woman, restoration of sight for the blind beggar, and an explanation of the tongues phenomenon for the Jerusalem crowd. The attention of their hearers was assured at the very *beginning* of their discourses.

Second, the communicators permitted no distractions. They skillfully redirected the attention of their listeners to the major truth they wished to present. As good teachers, they did not allow themselves to be sidetracked by irrelevant questions. Deviations were avoided, courteously but firmly. However, appropriate questions were answered and used to strengthen the learning experience of the audience.

Third, the discourses were well organized, factual, and comprehensible. The responsibility for decision was placed squarely upon the hearers—would they or would they not believe that Jesus was the Messiah? No obscure goals were pursued. Jesus Christ's identity was made clear. (Read John 4:25, 26; John 9:35-38; Acts 2:36, 37.)

Effective, clear declarations of Christian truths produce results especially when Christ is exalted as Saviour and Lord. He confronts the hearers with His challenge and His invitation to believe on Him. The wonder of it all is that the Holy Spirit speaks through human instruments in presenting Christ to the world!

Summary

Learning to communicate effectively through the medium of speaking requires a thorough understanding of the subject to be discussed as well as a burning desire to present it. The speaker should try to know his audience: their interests, needs, and prejudices. He must spend time in preparation, contemplation, prayer, and practice before He speaks. The best way of presenting the message should be followed. An informal, enthusiastic, and sincere speaking manner should be developed. He must remember that *personalized* communication is the type which Jesus, the Master Teacher, taught His messengers.

The apostles also used a simple, direct, and fearless manner in presenting the gospel. They spoke in the language of the people, started at their point of interest, and supported their statements by the Scriptures. They kept the audience's attention focused on major truths, presented Christ as Saviour, and terminated their discourses by urging action!

9 : Aids to Communication

The importance of the Christian message to the needs of mankind, the urgency of the time in which we now live, and the mandate from Christ to communicate this message throughout the world demand that we find the most effective means of transmitting the gospel. These means must be relevant, personalized, and practical.

Most people learn best when ideas are presented in a multisensory setting. This provides a means by which the data can be received into the brain with the greatest amount of reinforcement and perceptual reliability. In other words, if a person's mind can only see a symbol representing an idea, the chances of distorted perception of that symbol are greater than if he could also hear what the symbol represented. Therefore it is logical to conclude that the more sensory organs used in the perceptual process, the more accurate and extensive the knowledge acquired should be. As long as this form of input is synchronized and related to the experience of the receivers, it should be effective.

For example, the child who is being exposed to the idea of what a *dog* is will profit much more from actually *seeing* a dog, *hearing* him bark, and *touching* him than he would by seeing a picture of him. He would learn even less experientially about a dog by just listening to his mother describe in words what a dog is.

This is the basic purpose of teaching aids. They are

not intended as time fillers or adjuncts to a lesson, with a remote association to its central theme. Neither are they intended to dominate a presentation to the extent that people think of things rather than ideas or thoughts. We have not been called to communicate *things* but *truths*.

Teaching aids are intended to be as their name implies —*aids, helps, supplements* to a lesson. The teacher shows his pedagogical skill by selecting them wisely and using them properly. Such aids have no intrinsic value in themselves. It is the truth of God that has intrinsic value in Christian communications. It is God's message to man, originating with God Himself. Thus it has value within it, God-given value with power to save the souls of persons who accept it.

God has shown us by examples in His Word that He expects His message to be conveyed to man in the most effective way possible. This means that the intrinsic value of the message remains. Its truth does not change but the methods of presenting it may vary, and indeed must vary in order to give the receiver the best possible chance to *understand* it. Keeping these basic thoughts and principles in mind, a teacher can wisely use as aids some of the varied methods available to him in this technological age.

Types of Aids or Techniques

Audiovisual aids are now available to most teachers involved in Christian communications. Many of them are of excellent quality and provide valuable assistance to us. Filmstrips with records present Biblical stories and themes in a meaningful way. Projectors of all types are available, including even filmstrip projectors where light is provided by a kerosene lantern. These latter work very well in remote areas where electricity or batteries are not available, as I have learned from experience with them.

Sound movies and video tapes can be used for teacher

training especially, as well as for audiovisual exposure on the part of regular students. These aids can be rented or purchased by Christian educators. Film libraries are now becoming quite common in many districts, providing valuable rental services in audiovisual aids for many teachers.

The overhead projector is now a practical possibility for most Sunday schools. Transparencies are easily made and students find them to be attention-getters. Teachers can save a great deal of time by having their key ideas presented on transparencies, projecting them on the screen as they explain the points. This means that, with some ingenuity, a teacher can adapt a transparency to the needs of the class. The use of the overhead projector is preferred by many teachers to a chalkboard, as the teacher can look directly at the class while writing on the transparency as he talks. Transparencies can be prepared before class, saving the teacher from writing the material on the board. They also can be saved and filed for future reference.

The tape recorder is becoming increasingly popular, as its price is now within the capabilities of most church school budgets. The cassette type is now the most popular because it is so easy to use either for recording or playing. It has great versatility. For example, one suggestion for improving a person's ability to ask questions and thus to teach better, is to turn a tape recorder on at the beginning of a lesson and then have the teacher listen later to the teacher-class interaction in privacy. This experience can be helpful to a teacher provided that he concentrates on *one* major error at a time which he detects in his teaching from this exposure and tries to improve in that *one* area. Students also can improve their skill in reading or in discussion by using a tape recorder in a similar manner.

Cassette or reel tapes can be used to train a class to listen better, to speak more clearly, to learn from some well-known person more about God's Word, to derive benefit from some outstanding testimony of God's power working in another person's life, and so forth. They can be used as a communication link with missionaries in foreign lands to stimulate interest and concern. They can also be used in conjunction with slides or movies taken by the class members of a Christian drama which they have presented. Many young people today know how to make films, and this knowledge can be put to good use in furthering their interest in and knowledge of Biblical truths.

Discussion-type techniques can be very successful aids to communication. For younger children these discussion groups are usually directed by the teacher, who guides the children by skillful questioning to explore some new idea that has emerged from the lesson. Older children and adults can discuss in small groups, more or less carrying the social interaction and verbal exchange of ideas themselves, with minimal guidance from the teacher. However, these discussions should be carefully prepared in advance by having each topic assigned to specific groups the week before the proposed time for the discussion. This gives time for preparation so that a background of knowledge relative to the topic can be acquired. Otherwise discussion groups can deteriorate into just a "sharing of ignorance," as one teacher described it.

Panel discussions fall into the same category, as far as preparation is concerned. However, a panel usually consists of a few members of the class. The rest of the class listen to the panel members and then ask the panel questions on the topic discussed. Panel members are usually selected because they show interest in the subject and usually have more background experience upon which to draw. Panel discussion can be most enlightening to a class and a valuable help to the teacher because the members are encouraged to become "experts" in the field. The interest stimulated from this type of activity often can be very far-reaching in scope. Topics, of course, should be worthy of depth treatment and of interest to the class as a whole. There are many relevant topics today that can be effectively treated in this manner, such as "The Christian Viewpoint on Serving in the Armed Forces," "Bible Reading in the Schools," etc.

Debates can also be used occasionally by more mature students. With proper planning and supervision, children above the sixth grade level in school can participate in simple debates. Young people especially can debate more weighty subjects related to ethical or social problems or decisions. The emphasis should be on improving the students' understanding of the Christian position on a controversial subject, such as evolution, while at the same time understanding what the opposite opinions are and how they can be refuted by the Scriptures.

Projects are good for increasing pupil involvement and interest in learning. They also help pupils to apply what they are learning to everyday practical experiences. Some persons enjoy immensely this type of learning activity because although they may not be verbally oriented, they do learn a great deal from working with their hands or engaging in some type of action program. This is, indeed, more than "busy work" without educational goals. Projects should be carefully planned in view of the specific goals of the unit of study in which the class is involved. It is advisable to decide at the beginning of a new unit of study what types of projects are practical and feasible. Teacher-pupil planning, especially for older children and adults, should be encouraged. Often brainstorming with definite goals in mind can be very beneficial. Involving the students in the planning stages will stimulate interest in projects related to community needs, overseas appeals, church projects already underway, and various personal needs of elderly or handicapped persons of the Christian community. Sometimes these projects can be correlated with other group activities of the Royal Rangers, Missionettes, Men's Ministries, Women's Missionary Council, or Christ's Ambassadors.

Younger children enjoy handcraft and in fact often benefit considerably from involving themselves in projects of this type. These projects, if planned and executed properly (which means that the children do the projects and complete them rather than the teacher) can be valuable learning aids. Older children will often be willing to undertake more sophisticated projects such as replicas of the Ark, the Tabernacle, or the Manger Scene, or a modern scene such as an African village reproduced from a missionary's slide. Drawings and paintings of Biblical stories or Christian events in the world today can often be very rewarding, not only to the students but to their parents and other adults who take an interest in the Christian education of the young.

Games are often used to stimulate interest and to reinforce learning in many schools today. Learning can be fun, involving the full attention of the student. Games should, of course, fulfill educational goals. They do not have to be complicated but are frequently simple devices in which motivational aids are built in. For example, as we have previously discussed, many students are not familiar with the language of the Bible. A game to teach Biblical vocabulary could be devised in which the key words of a series of lessons are printed on cards (3- by 5-inch filing cards). Other cards of a different color would have the definitions or another word meaning the same as the key word printed on them.

After the cards have been shuffled, they should be distributed, with each team having the same number of key word cards as matched meaning cards. Team A would have the first opportunity to call out a key word which one of its members has, challenging Team B to match it with the right definition or synonym. A point is scored for Team B if someone on the team produces the matching card. If no one does produce the card in the time allotted, and a member of Team A can successfully present the winning match, Team A receives two points. Ordinarily not more than 10 minutes should be allotted for this type of activity, preferably at the end of the period. This type of vocabulary game can be played in a variety of ways but it should always be preceded by a time of studying the pronunciation and meanings of the key words (suggested in Chapter 7 under readiness activities).

Games should primarily be means of reinforcing knowledge already learned. Overlearning for retention is one of the major goals of this teaching aid to better communication. At the same time it can be a pleasurable means of attaining this goal and prevent loss of attention on the part of students.

Quiz games can be used as basic review, with time given for preparation on the part of the class members. Extrinsic rewards may or may not be used in this situation, depending on the judgment of the teacher. Children from deprived areas often need extrinsic rewards to motivate them to learn, until they really become interested in knowing Biblical truth because of the intrinsic value which they receive. For children who know the joy of learning, often the approval of the teacher and their fellow class members is adequate reward.

The church library or class library should be an essential and much used vehicle of learning. Take time to let your class visit the library, showing them how to use it and introducing new books to them periodically. One enterprising teacher started a library for her class by asking each child to try to earn money during the week to buy one Christian paperback book. As soon as sufficient money was collected to buy a variety of these paperbacks, each child was asked to select one to read (the teacher and some parents had given money to buy additional copies). The books were kept in circulation by adhering to the rule that each child would be allowed to keep a book for only a week. Children began to discuss the books in class. The teacher found books an asset in her individual conferences with the children when she listened to them read a special selection that each had chosen to share with the teacher. Sometimes time was found for a child to read part of a book to other class members.

This type of communication can be a great asset in developing a lifetime interest in good Christian literature. It can be used to strengthen the child's faith in God. For children who come from non-Christian homes, it may be the tool that will open their minds and hearts to Christ. For adolescents, reading Christian literature can be therapeutic and challenging. Biographies of famous Christians can inspire them to consider God's call for their own lives. More mature readers often find books written by evangelical scholars thought-provoking and stimulating. Even a small church should be able to start a library containing a variety of Christian literature that will be of interest to the entire constituency.

Bible study courses are now becoming more accessible to the general Christian public through correspondence and are becoming increasingly popular. Christian newspapers and magazines, which feature new types of styles, provide a world view of Christian happenings and challenges.

The types of teaching or learning aids used will depend on the levels of experience of the learners, their interests, learning styles, and needs. Top priority should be given to the spiritual needs of the students, involving them as much as possible in the learning process. Spiritual understanding can be increased and the entire communication cycle improved by the efficient use of instructional and motivational aids.

Examples of Use of Aids

In our electronic age research has indicated that mass media techniques are limited in their effectiveness for changing basic attitudes of the public. Personal contact by a credible teacher adds the needed personal touch to communication. This gives opportunity for the presented message in filmstrip, movie, tape recording, pictorial aid, dramatized production, project display, or other audiovisual aid to be applied to the individual needs of the students. In other words, the touch of the skillful, insightful teacher will always be needed to *personalize* the communicated message. Jesus Himself highlighted this truth.

A modern-day example of the impact of audiovisual aids on the communication of the gospel message is the tremendous number of conversions to Christ that have resulted from the screen productions sponsored by the Billy Graham Evangelistic Association and other evangelical institutions. However, it should be noted that the follow-up programs of these conversions involve personal communication at the individual level. Thousands of dedicated Christian teachers and workers have engaged in these activities, which are a very important part of effective stewardship. Although this type of activity is often not publicized, its value is not overlooked by Christ. The truth remains that teaching aids are tools, often very effective tools. But the teacher is the craftsman who must know *when* and *how* to use the tools under the direction and guidance of the Holy Spirit.

Summary

A great number of new types of media are available to the communicator today. A wise teacher knows how to use teachings aids that are a part of the environment in which his students live, just as Jesus did in His day. The concerned teacher also knows how to use materials and techniques that have proven valuable in the communication of ideas from one mind to another in this day of electronics and technology. It is no longer necessary to depend on only one medium to communicate Christ's message nor to limit oneself to techniques that have been overworked and no longer appeal to learners.

Because of the importance of communicating the gospel message in the best possible manner for different types of learners, the Christian communicator must always seek to use the best medium at hand as an aid to communication. At the same time, one does not forget the *purpose* of Christian communication and overemphasize the *means*. God did not call His messengers to be entertaining babysitters, seeking only to pacify people. On the other hand, God does not want us to be so boring that learning is minimal. Let us find the best aid for each teaching opportunity and use it purposefully.

10 : Teacher-Pupil Communications

There is a great need for models of Christian life-styles today. In many homes children do not see a model of Christian living. The chances are remote that they will encounter one in school. Often, sad to say, they do not find one in church. Christian teachers need to remember that children learn to love God, one another, and adults in their lives by imitation and example. They learn also how to communicate with others by demonstration and practice. This is true of all human beings, not just children.

Teacher Accountability

The teacher may know how to communicate effectively the message of Jesus Christ through the verbal medium. Does he also know how to communicate this message by his daily living? "Faith without works is dead," James wrote. Faith with works is tremendously powerful, directing the receivers' attention to spiritual reality as it is presented in word and in deed. All of us know that this is true.

In secular education this is called the decade of teacher accountability. Will it also be the decade of accountability for Christian communicators? Can we develop a greater sensitivity to God's view in this matter at a time when our society seems to us to be more and more oriented toward irresponsibility? It is only logical to expect that a secular society which has eliminated God from its thinking would become increasingly arrogant. After all, to whom should man be responsible if there is no God in this universe? This is, indeed, the result of secular thinking, but Christians cannot conform to this mold of thinking. God's Word is clear that we are accountable for what we do with our own souls as well as what we do *to* and *for* the souls of others for whom we are responsible.

Today in education there is much discussion concerning the pros and cons of performance contracts. Certain companies have been assigned by the Federal Government of the United States to carry out these contracts with selected school systems across the country. These educational companies promise that each child entrusted to their instructional care shall make satisfactory progress in learning, especially in the basic communication skills like the three R's, as we commonly call them. In this type of program, the teacher is being held accountable along with his supervisors and consultants for children's learning. If the learner is not motivated to learn, the teacher must find out the reasons. If he has a handicap, preventing him from learning in the way that normal children do, the teacher must find out the best way that he does receive information, and teach him using that channel of communication. Other children have no desire to learn because there is no person, according to their thinking, who really cares whether they learn or not. The teacher must show that he cares enough to be patient and that he is concerned for all children in the class, including the unmotivated ones.

Pressure is mounting in many large cities of America to place teachers under the obligation to sign performance contracts. The public is agitating for the upgrading of public schools. Meanwhile, problems facing educators are disconcerting in many areas owing to the widespread use of drugs, disrespect for adults, school vandalism and violence, racial prejudice, and civil disobedience. However, in spite of all these difficulties which make teaching a hazardous occupation, many teachers are willing to sign contracts of accountability, provided that they have the cooperation of the communities in which they teach.

Although Christian teachers and parents may likewise feel that there are many problems associated with successful communication with the young, they need not despair, for they have a source of divine wisdom and expertise upon which to draw. However, the willingness and the concern to be accountable for each pupil's progress in learning spiritual truths should be very evident among Christian teachers and parents. Whether the learning laboratory is at home, school, or church, we are indeed accountable before God for the children and young people entrusted to our care. Are we willing to "contract" with God, depending on His divine help, that we shall communicate His truth to our children in a responsible manner in both word and deed?

In the Old Testament, Moses instructed the Israelites, before they entered the Promised Land, to settle and establish homes, and to always remember their God-given responsibility to teach their children God's Law and truth. They were to be responsible for relating the history of God's miraculous care of His people as they left Egypt's bondage and journeyed in the wilderness and desert on their circuitous way to Canaan. This historical heritage was unique because it was God-centered and therefore was important. Moses stated that its preservation for future generations would be assured if the Israelites obeyed God and taught their children and grandchildren.

Furthermore, these parents were to be living examples to their children that they believed in God by keeping His commandments and by worshiping Him in sincerity and devotion. They were responsible for their actions as well as their words. They were to teach in word and in deed the revelation of God which He wanted communicated to their children and grandchildren.

When Israel failed to keep these instructions and allowed their children to transgress God's Law, God reprimanded them by allowing their enemies to subjugate them and afflict them. Likewise, God has given us these historical truths to show us that He expects us to be accountable to Him for what we teach, how we teach it, and how well we live His revealed truth before our children.

How Can Teachers Be Responsible Communicators?

The Christian communicator, who is often a teacher, needs to show the child how to listen by being a good listener himself. He shows a student how to study by providing a good model of study habits and techniques in his own personal life. He believes that one not only must listen to God's Word but be a doer of it. He looks in the mirror of God's Word daily and sees himself as God perceives him. He does not forget what he has been shown by God, but by God's grace applies remedial measures to his character and behavior. He teaches his students to respect people by first of all showing respect for the pupil himself. A child who does not feel any self-respect because of poor relationships with adults in his home will only learn to respect himself, as a person created by God, as the teacher respects him. The teacher who develops meaningful relationships with his children does this out of respect for them as God's handiwork. He then lovingly believes that they will change when they give their hearts to Christ.

It is indeed true, as Francis Schaeffer has stated in *Pollution and the Death of Man: The Christian View of Ecology*, that if we love God, we will love His creation and treat man and nature with integrity. A child who has learned to respect himself as God's creation will be more likely to respond to the Christian concept of sin and salvation.

A wise teacher shows his pupils how to open their hearts to Christ in confidence and faith. Then he provides opportunities at the appropriate time for personal encounters with Christ. This type of application of divine truth to personal reality is very important. We must impress on our students that this decision is a personal one of great significance. They are not only being asked to give their *hearts* to Christ, believing in Him as their Saviour; they are being presented with an opportunity to give their *lives* to Christ. Our children can realize how much it means to Jesus to redeem them because it means so much to us. The joy, flooding our souls because of their repentance and regeneration, is representative of Christ's great joy in being able to forgive them, to receive them as His children, and to write their names in the Book of Life.

The Christian teacher is also accountable for perhaps the most difficult task of all. Whether he is a parent or an educator entrusted with the responsibility of teaching others, part of that accountability includes nurturing the newborn child of God in the love and knowledge of the Lord. Developing maturity is not an easy matter, as Paul noted in his relationships with the Corinthian Church. One of the great problems Paul had in communicating the truth to them was their limited receptivity. They were limited in ability to take in the Word of God because they were concentrating on the *messenger* instead of the *message* (1 Cor. 1:12).

While developing maturity in our students, we ourselves must be growing people. The basis of this spiritual growth is continuous knowledge of Jesus Christ, obedience to that knowledge (walking in the light), and continuing to share this knowledge or light with others. The influence of a caring teacher who is mature in Christian experience and character can never be fully appraised. This caring person shares his maturity with the persons to whom he is communicating humbly, so that constantly the observers perceive the reality of the message. Then, as they become more mature themselves, they will concentrate less on the messenger and more on the kernels of spiritual truth found in the message.

The Christian teacher must also believe that persons who have been greatly influenced by his ministry and teaching will continue to grow in knowledge and truth, even though they are removed from his immediate influence. This is part of the pain of growing up—the separation of the parent from the child, the teacher from the student. We must believe, however, in the faithfulness of the Holy Spirit to bring to the remembrance of the children, no matter where they might be, the basic concepts of God's Word that we have tried to communicate to them by word and by example. We must believe that, no matter what influences may surround them as they become independent and "fly on their own," God's Word will accomplish its work in their lives. We must believe that the model of Christian living that we have tried, by God's grace, to show them will help "shore up" their faith in Christ, keeping them growing, and reaching out for more and more of God's truth.

The Pupil Communicates

Communications involve people responding to the message and reacting to the messenger. The transmitter must be quick to detect, with a fair degree of accuracy, whether or not the message is being received correctly. The more involved a receiver becomes in thinking about the message, associating it with past experiences, categorizing the key ideas, refraining from evaluation until a genuine effort has been made to understand what the message is, the better he will be able to respond to it. Communication becomes a two-way channel as the receiver and transmitter reverse roles and the latter has the opportunity to discover whether or not his message has been understood.

Channels of feedback to the alert transmitter or teacher assist him in knowing the extent to which his communication goals have been realized. Sometimes the channels of pupil response may be activities other than simple questions for clarification. They may involve the pupils in drama, role playing, pantomiming, explaining to other students what they have learned, expressing interpretations of the ideas transmitted, writing poems or essays based on the topic discussed, or reading to the class material which sheds new light on the topic. All of these activities will help the learners to learn more from the communications process and remember more of the ideas presented.

The ones who remembered best what Jesus said that day were the ones who had a positive reaction to Jesus' announcement. Jesus became in reality spiritual bread, sustaining their souls, satisfying their hunger to know God in truth. Here the accountability of the listener-pupil becomes apparent. One becomes responsible for his reaction to truth. He can no longer say, "I did not know." Exposure to God's truth poses an obligation for eternity on the receiver. Those Jews in Jesus' audience that day in Galilee could no longer plead ignorance of who Jesus was. He had told them plainly.

Research has indicated that if the teacher's mind-set is similar to that of the students or the students' to the teacher's, much more learning results from the communication. For example, if the teacher's emphasis in the cognitive domain (that of knowledge, being able to deal with concepts) is factually oriented, the students whose minds are also factually oriented will remember many of the facts which the teacher has presented. However, if the teacher believes strongly that students should be able to conceptualize beyond the facts presented, the ones who will benefit the most from his discourse will be the students oriented toward a higher conceptual level of thinking.

Communicating ideas from person to person is a difficult and often precarious venture. The best success will be realized when what the teacher wants a student to learn and what the student wants to learn are compatible or similar. The more divergent the students' views are from the teacher's, the less chance there is of understanding and action. Of course, in Christian education and communication we depend on the Holy Spirit to change the mind-set of listeners so that they become more receptive to the message. Hostile pupils affect adversely a listening situation, often threatening to break the communication entirely. We have seen quite dramatic demonstrations of this fact in recent years, especially on college campuses. Pupil communication, involving response and constructive action, to a transmitted message must be accountable and responsible. It implies integrity on the part of the receiver as well as the transmitter. It means respect for the teacher or communicator as one of God's creation. Love for God implies love for man whom God has made in His image.

Imperfections in teachers need to be expected by pupils because teachers are human. Pupils should act constructively to remedy the teacher's imperfections in the spirit of love and mutual respect. Teachers also must bear with the imperfections of their students, encouraging them to change and strive for improvement. All things are possible with God. We must avoid labelling people or expecting no change to take place, thus raising formidable barriers to communicating the gospel of Jesus Christ.

Learning to Apply Truth

Receivers, such as pupils, are persons who learn as all persons do by percept, example, and action. They learn to worship God, to enjoy communion with Him, to engage in prayer and thanksgiving by understanding the function of these spiritual exercises. They also learn by observing an experienced Christian who practices these expressions of Christian devotion. The final step of learning involves actual practice on the part of the learners in these activities. Christian students learn in this manner *how* to communicate with God.

Pupils learn the value of confession of sin and wrongdoing by perceiving rationally or intuitively why this activity is important to achieving the major goal of forgiveness and relief from guilt. Then they learn by the example of mature Christian teachers who are not afraid to confess their faults to one another. The final step is the sincere application of this truth to the pupil's individual experience, when he confesses *what is really* bothering him, not sidestepping the basic issue between him and God. The truth of confession and forgiveness becomes reality for him.

Pupils learn to share Christ in the same manner. They learn concepts of divine reality through communication, integrating them into their experiential knowledge by applying them to their daily living. In most cases where this is done, you will find somewhere a responsible parent, teacher, or other influential communicator who has demonstrated by his life *how* the concept of Christian truth can be translated into daily living and sharing with others. This person shows by his example a model of Christian witnessing. Eventually the learner will be able to follow Christ uniquely and depend more and more on Him as the true Model and Leader. He becomes a responsible receiver of God's truth, recognizing his accountability to receive the message from God in humility and thanksgiving. Then he is well on his way toward becoming in turn an accountable communicator, sharing what he knows of God's revealed truth to other persons.

Summary

The message of God becomes an integral part of human living, influencing many lives, living forever in receivers' minds as they become personally involved in responding both in word and deed to God's revealed truth. The stimulus for this type of profitable communication is initially a model, a human messenger whom God has made accountable to Him for instructing and living the truth—literally walking in the light daily. As the pupil-receivers become more mature in Christian experience, they are able to look beyond the messenger to the message. The message reveals Christ to them so that the object of their attention becomes Christ, the perfect Model of Christian living, rather than the imperfect model of the teacher or communicator of the message.

The willingness of the teacher to be responsible for his pupils' learning and growth in Christian reality and experience is a key factor in teacher-pupil communications. Pupils under the guidance of credible, knowledgeable, dedicated teachers who really care for God's creation because they love God, will, by God's grace and power, become in time effective communicators of God's message to their own generation. They in turn will develop the accountability necessary to become effective transmitters of the gospel of Jesus Christ because they have learned to be responsible learners.

Bibliography

Asimor, Isaac. "Our Race with Doom." *T.V. Guide,* June 5-11, 1971.

Dennett, H. *Christian Communications in a Changing World.* London: Victory Press, 1968.

Henry, Carl. *Faith at the Frontiers.* Chicago: Moody Press, 1969.

Jones, E. Stanley. *The Mastery of Life.* London: Hodder & Stoughton, 1956.

Lewis, C.S. "On Moving with the Times." *Christianity Today,* March 26, 1971.

Miller, George A. *The Psychology of Communication.* London: Penguin Press, 1968

Schaeffer, Francis A. *Death in the City.* Downers Grove, Ill.: Intervarsity Press, 1969.

Staton, Thomas F. *How to Study.* Nashville: McQuiddy Printing Co., 1962.

Stowe, Everett M. *Communicating Reality Through Symbols.* Philadelphia: Westminster Press, 1966.

Tournier, Paul. *The Whole Person in a Broken World.* New York: Harper & Row, 1964.

Explanations:

Taylor's paraphrase of the New Testament was used in quotations from the New Testament for clarity.

Antoinette Goetschius' poem was reprinted in the Gold Star Album, Valley Forge, Arthur DeMoss, Publisher, 1971. It was originally printed in the Feb. 18, 1948, issue of *The Christian Century.*